Pat Williams' Tales from the
PHILADELPHIA
76ERS

Pat Williams
with Gordon Jones

Foreword by Billy Cunningham

SportsPublishingLLC.com

ISBN 13: 978-1-59670-117-5

Publishers: Peter L. Bannon and Joseph J. Bannon Sr.
Senior managing editor: Susan M. Moyer
Acquisitions editor: John Humenik
Editor: Jennine Crucet
Art director: Dustin J. Hubbart
Dust jacket design: Joseph Brumleve
Interior layout: Rachel Hubbart
Photo editor: Jessica Martinich

Sports Publishing L.L.C.
804 North Neil Street
Champaign, IL 61820
Phone: 1-877-424-2665
Fax: 217-363-2073
www.SportsPublishingLLC.com

Printed in the United States of America

CIP data available upon request

This book is enthusiastically dedicated to the sports fans of the Philadelphia area—the most rabid rooters in the country—and to Hall of Famer Phil Jasner, a veteran *Philadelphia Daily News* NBA writer and a living legend in pro basketball.

—Pat Williams

To Ryan Jones, my favorite author, and to Barbara Jones, my favorite desk "guy."

—Gordon Jones

CONTENTS

FOREWORD

By the spring of 2007, my dear friend Jim Hudock was fading.

We'd overlapped for a single year at the University of North Carolina—1961-62—when I was a freshman and he a senior (and Dean Smith's first captain). A native of Northeastern Pennsylvania, he had put down roots in the Tar Heel State, becoming a dentist in Kinston.

Now, sadly, cancer was having its way with him; it would take his life in May. During one of our final conversations, I had to ask him: What are the most important things in life, as you see it?

He couldn't answer at that particular moment. He was too overwhelmed by the question.

But when we next spoke he said that when the end grows near, you again come to understand that the things that really matter are the things that should have mattered all along: family, friends, and religious faith. You cling to others, and you cling to something larger than yourself.

As wonderful as the Philadelphia 76ers' 1982-83 season was, the things I treasure most are the relationships I had (and have) with that very special group of men.

Now, more than ever, I appreciate the way the majority of them persevered through years of disappointment. Now, more than ever, I cherish the love and respect they had for each other, the sacrifices they made, and the unselfishness and sense of purpose they displayed.

That team had great talent, sure: two Hall of Famers in Julius Erving and Moses Malone; two near-Hall of Famers in Maurice Cheeks and Bobby Jones; one would-be Hall of Famer in Andrew Toney. But talent only goes so far. There needs to be a commitment to each other, and to a common goal.

I had seen that when I played alongside Wilt Chamberlain with the Sixers. When we won the 1966-67 championship, it was because Wilt sacrificed some scoring to concentrate on other things. That allowed the talents of our other great players, like Hal Greer, Chet Walker, Luke Jackson, and Wali Jones, to emerge.

It was the same in '82-83. No one was concerned with individual goals. Everyone wanted what was best for the team. Julius, who had carried so much of the load for so many years, was happy to have someone like Moses alongside him. Moses, who had excelled in Houston, was happy to blend in. All our other players understood and embraced their roles.

That was a team that for years had come so close, losing in the Finals in 1977 (the year before I became the coach), as well as in '80 and '82, and also losing to Boston in the '81 Eastern Conference Finals after taking a three-games-to-one lead.

That last one was the hardest for me to take. Both teams had won a league-best 62 games during the regular season. Both knew the series was for the world championship, and both approached it that way. But we lost those last three games by a total of five points. It took me a long time to get over it.

Eventually, though, you have to move on. You stop beating yourself up. You stop feeling sorry for yourself. You stop blaming referees or cursing your luck. You just have to ask yourself: What did I learn from that situation? And then you start climbing the mountain again.

Our whole team adopted the same approach, and I've often thought it admirable the way our players took something positive out of a negative situation and kept pushing, year after year.

It took a bold stroke by Harold Katz in September 1982—the acquisition of Moses—to put us over the top. I had a chance to sit down with Moses in a hotel in New York City the night we signed him to an offer sheet, and I felt quite certain he would blend in well with our team.

But we had to give up Caldwell Jones to get him. Veterans like Darryl Dawkins, Steve Mix, Mike Bantom, and Lionel Hollins had also departed. The remaining players were upset over losing their friends. But when they arrived at training camp, got to know Moses, and realized how great an impact he could have on the court, everything fell into place.

It was a dream season, the story of which is recreated in this book. Pat Williams, who as the Sixers' general manager helped put this team together, and Gordie Jones, who covered the season, take us on the entire, joyous journey, from its beginnings in a hotel suite in New York City (where we signed Moses to an offer sheet), to its end in Veterans Stadium (where the celebratory parade concluded). Along the way we revisit familiar sites. We are reintroduced to old friends and rivals. And we relive one of the finest seasons in pro basketball history.

Again, we are reminded how everybody stuck together, at the way everybody understood they were part of something larger than themselves.

I cherish that year. But more than that, I cherish everything that made it possible.

Billy Cunningham
76ers head coach, 1977-85
November 2007

INTRODUCTION

It was seemingly just another July day at beautiful Duncan Park in Spartanburg, South Carolina. It was 1968, and I was in my fourth year as the president and general manager of the Phillies' minor league affiliate in the Western Carolinas League. The league's All-Star Game was being played in our ballpark that night.

As I walked to my desk in our cramped offices, I noticed that my secretary, Claire Johns, had left a handwritten note by my phone. The message was from a Jack Ramsay in Inglewood, California. The Jack Ramsay who I had watched coach at the Palestra all those years ago, the Jack Ramsay who was general manager of the Philadelphia 76ers?

I returned the call, and Jack answered at his hotel room. I had never met the man, but he explained to me he was there in Inglewood to trade Wilt Chamberlain to the Lakers. He also told me Alex Hannum was not returning as the Sixers coach, and he himself was taking over in addition to his work as the GM. He needed someone to run the day-to-day operation of the front office. Would I be interested? Would I come to Philadelphia to talk about it?

I had always been a great basketball follower, but I had never thought for one minute about a career in the NBA. All of my goals and dreams were to get to the major leagues in baseball. Nothing had ever opened up in baseball to that point, so I figured why not go and talk?

After two trips to Philadelphia to visit with Jack and owner Irv Kosloff, I was offered the position of business manager—a three-year deal, $20,000 a year. It was the largest contract I had ever heard of in my life! (I had been making $800 a month in Spartanburg.)

I resigned my position in Spartanburg and joined the Sixers for the Wilt-less 1968-69 season. In the summer of 1969, I was contacted by the Chicago Bulls to serve as their general manager. I was 29 years old, and the Sixers agreed to release me from my contract if I would agree to a deal Jack wanted to make—forward Chet Walker to the Bulls for forward Jimmy Washington. Sounded good to me.

I signed a two-year deal with Chicago, at $30,000 a year. Things were looking up. I had four wonderful years building the Bulls, and I left in the summer of 1973 to become GM of the Atlanta Hawks.

After trading Pete Maravich to New Orleans in May 1974, I heard from my friend Irv Kosloff, still the Sixers' owner. Things were at low tide in Philadelphia. The team was struggling back from the infamous 9-73 finish in '72-73. First-round pick Marvin Barnes had refused to sign with the Sixers, choosing instead to flee to the ABA. The GM post was open, and Irv asked me to come and help rebuild the team.

I was thrilled to return to my home area, but certainly cognizant of the enormous task that lay ahead. It would be nearly a decade before everything would be in place, allowing us to take the final, spectacular step to a championship.

The stories you're about to read are all part of the pulsating account of our 1982-83 title season. Longtime Philadelphia-area sportswriter Gordie Jones and I have done hundreds of interviews for this project. We have spoken to every member of that team, as well as scores of NBA players, referees, writers, broadcasters, fans, and spouses. We haven't left any stone unturned.

Sit back. Get ready for the ride. Enjoy, once more, the last major championship the city of Philadelphia has celebrated. Hard to believe it was 25 years ago. But as you read this book, it will seem like yesterday.

Pat Williams
November 2007

1

Maurice Cheeks never dunked. Sure, Harvey Pollack—the Philadelphia 76ers' ageless, tireless stat guy—could unearth a dog-eared play-by-play sheet indicating otherwise. Harvey always kept track of stuff like that. That, and everything else.

But in most people's minds, our point guard never dunked. That wasn't him. He did his job quietly and efficiently, hiding from the spotlight while making everybody else look good. Only occasionally would he emerge from the sizable shadows cast by his more-celebrated teammates—Moses Malone, Julius Erving, Andrew Toney, et al.—to make a timely steal, a deft pass, a clutch jumper. But then he would disappear again. It was easy to forget about him.

That changed late on the night of May 31, 1983.

Game 4 of the NBA Finals had been decided. The Los Angeles Lakers, gallant but gimpy, were done. We were about to finish off a sweep, in the process nearly fulfilling Malone's pre-playoff prognostication: "Fo', fo', fo'." In Moses-speak, that meant the Sixers were going to sweep three best-of-seven series en route to the championship.

And we came close, excusing the New York Knicks in fo', and the Milwaukee Bucks in five. And now the Lakers were about to be dismissed.

Erving—Dr. J—had seen to that, with the seven-point fourth-quarter flurry that put the Sixers, down by 11 points after three, ahead for good.

Just a few seconds remained when Cheeks rebounded Magic Johnson's missed three-pointer near the foul line and started high-stepping downcourt. He never did that, either.

Nor, it seemed, did he ever fail to give Erving the ball. But now Julius was running alongside him, on his left. Surely on this night of all nights, on a night when Doc would win the title everyone felt he so richly deserved, Cheeks would afford one of history's greatest dunkers the opportunity to provide an exclamation point.

Only Maurice never saw him. That has always been his story, and he has stuck to it. He was still high-stepping; somebody later said it looked as if he were riding a hobby horse. The Doctor, wearing a bemused expression, was reduced to spectator as Cheeks stormed to the rim. For a moment Lakers defensive stopper Michael Cooper rose as if to challenge him, then thought better of it.

So Maurice Cheeks—the guy who never dunked, the guy who never wanted to be noticed—dunked. And the celebration began.

ROOTS

Where should we begin? In 1972-73, when the Sixers—the 9-73 Sixers—were not just the worst team in basketball, but one of the worst teams in the history of organized sports? In 1976, when Dr. J arrived? How about the summer of 1977, when, after losing to Portland in the Finals, we launched the "We Owe You One" ad campaign? Or how about after each subsequent playoff disappointment, each new IOU?

Maybe none of the above. Maybe it's best to begin with a phone call from Harold Katz, the team's owner, to the suburban Philadelphia home of our assistant general manager, John Nash, on the night of Sunday, August 29, 1982. Katz, Nash remembers, was calling from a casino in Las Vegas. Katz recalls he was on a family outing in Lake Tahoe.

Whatever the case, his message to Nash was clear: Get in touch with Moses Malone's people. Let's have a meeting. Let's try to sign Moses.

We had traded our center, Darryl Dawkins, to New Jersey two days earlier—a deal I didn't hear about until well after the fact, since I was touring China with a group of NBA players headed by Julius Erving. This being long before cell phones, word didn't reach me until someone tracked me down at a hotel in Hong Kong. I passed the news along to the rest of our traveling party, which included M.L. Carr, the impish, towel-waving reserve forward for the Boston Celtics.

"Looks like Red just lit another cigar," Carr said.

Certainly Celtics icon Red Auerbach had savored his share of victory cigars at our expense over the years. But something other than cigar smoke was in the air.

CENTER OF ATTENTION

We had been having conversations about possible replacements for Darryl for the better part of the month. Denver center Dan Issel was a free agent. So was Seattle's Jack Sikma. But in Harold's mind, the most logical choice was Moses; he was the ultimate hard hat, a winner of three rebounding titles and two MVP awards in his six seasons in Houston. Few have ever been so skilled at working the offensive glass, at reducing a difficult task like rebounding to its simplest terms.

"There's only one ball," Malone said in 2006, "so go get it."

Which was a slight variation on the job description he had provided years before: "I turn, and I go to the rack."

Pressed for a more complete explanation one time by a Rockets teammate, guard Mike Dunleavy, Malone said it was a matter of simple math: "Suppose there are 100 rebounds in a game. I'm going after all 100, and 15 will fall into my hands."

"Pretty simple, but true," Dunleavy said years later. "Moses wasn't the greatest athlete in the league. He didn't have huge hands, and he wasn't a great leaper. But he worked so hard. His effort was off the charts, proving if you try your hardest all the time, there's no telling where you might end up. You'll surprise yourself sometimes."

Moses had been the first high school player to bypass college, leaping right from a hardscrabble neighborhood in Petersburg, Virginia—The Heights—to Utah of the ABA in 1974. An immediate star, his teammates called him "Superkid." A radio guy was less kind; hearing Malone's truncated speech pattern, he labeled him "Mumbles."

The ABA folded after Moses' second season, 1975-76, and Portland scooped him up in the dispersal draft. But these were the Trail Blazers of Bill Walton and Maurice Lucas, a team that would go on to beat us in that year's Finals. They had no interest in paying a backup center in excess of $300,000, so they traded Moses to Buffalo for a first-round draft pick.

"They should have kept Moses, and traded me," Walton said in 2006—

and indeed, Walton's feet betrayed him soon after the Blazers' title run, preventing him from having the career he might have otherwise enjoyed.

Once Buffalo acquired Moses, the club turned around and sent him to Houston for two first-round choices. And it was there that his career took flight. His teammates took to calling him "Mo-zilla," because, like Godzilla, he would "come to town and tear the place up," as one of them, Bill Willoughby, recalled.

In 1980-81, Moses led a 40-42 Rockets team to the NBA Finals. And once there, he claimed he and four guys from his neighborhood could beat the lordly Celtics. The Rockets, alas, could not; Boston won in six games.

Del Harris coached that team, having succeeded Tom Nissalke in 1979. Harris had also worked under Nissalke in Utah, when Moses broke in, and as a result understood Malone was a much better athlete than most people believed; on a dare he once touched his forehead to the rim during practice. But Moses seldom made one spectacular leap during games, choosing instead to go up once, twice, a third time—whatever it took, the result being that he seemed to be in constant orbit.

Moses was equally shrewd in off-court matters. One summer, he was part of a group of American players accompanying Nissalke and Harris to the Dominican Republic. No one wanted the local currency, so Harris, who speaks Spanish, arranged to exchange it for American money.

The deal was made in Nissalke's hotel room, and as Harris recalled, with a guy who brought a suitcase full of cash—and a bodyguard. The bodyguard sat across the room, a pistol on the table in front of him, and oversaw the transaction.

Harris later ran into Malone, who had made a deal on his own, a better deal than the one Harris had made, as it turned out. Why, Del asked Moses, had he gone ahead and done it so quickly?

"I don't want no money that doesn't have George Washington's picture on it," he said.

LATE ARRIVAL

We wanted to give Moses piles of money with George Washington's picture on it. But John Nash wasn't able to reach Moses' attorneys, Lee Fentress and David Falk, until the morning after he took Harold's call. Nash also found out that Billy Cunningham, our coach, was on a golf course in North Carolina—Pinehurst No. 2—so he called down there and had someone track him down.

The decision was made to convene a meeting at the Grand Hyatt in New York City on Tuesday night at seven, since Moses was leaving out of New York the following morning, bound for Europe with a group of NBA stars on a Nike-sponsored trip.

When the appointed hour rolled around, everyone was present in Katz's suite: Harold and his attorney, Lawrence Shaiman; Nash; Fentress, Falk and two other attorneys; Moses and his wife, Alfreda.

Everyone but Billy Cunningham.

He had caught a flight to Newark, New Jersey, and was told cab fare from there to New York was $70. He took the bus instead—for $7—and later that night, after all sorts of astronomical dollar figures had been tossed around, told Katz that if nothing else, at least he had saved his owner $63.

But he was an hour late. There was, Nash recalled, tension in the room; serious negotiations could not commence until Billy sat down with Moses and determined if he would be willing to blend in with Doc and the rest of our players. Could he adapt to a fast-paced style after playing for a walk-it-up team in Houston?

They spoke for the better part of an hour, and Billy was satisfied that there would be no clash of egos.

"What does that word mean, 'Ego'?" Moses asked, years later. "I left all my ego on the playground." Then he laughed.

"They were a great team before I got here, so I just came to be part of the puzzle," he recalled. "I knew when I got here it was Dr. J's team. It was not Moses Malone's team. Doc was the guy here. Doc is the leader, so you've got to follow the leader. You've got a lot of Indians, but you've got to have chiefs somewhere."

After meeting with Billy, Moses and Alfreda departed the suite. Negotiations began with Harold as the point man.

"Actually it was a very easy deal to make, because they wanted $2 million a year for Moses, which was giant money then," Katz remembered.

And none of that money was to be deferred, as Moses had made clear in his conversations with Harold, before he departed.

"He must have told me ten times, 'No 'ferred, no 'ferred'," Katz said.

It was nearly 2 a.m. when a verbal agreement was reached—six years and $13.2 million (including a $1 million signing bonus)—which would make Moses the highest-paid player in the game. Shaiman put everything in writing, and copies were made in the hotel's business office when it opened at six. Then everyone signed it.

"In terms of excitement," Nash said, "that night in the Grand Hyatt might have been the most exciting night I've ever had in sports."

IMMEDIATE BUZZ

Two days later, our party landed in LaGuardia. We passed a newsstand and saw the screaming headlines about the Sixers signing Moses to an offer sheet. M.L. Carr saw them, too.

"Looks like that cigar just went out," Julius told him.

When word reached Sixers forward Earl Cureton, he called his friend and teammate, Andrew Toney, in Louisiana.

"Go get your ring size measured," Earl told him.

CLAUSE AND EFFECT

The offer sheet was delivered to the Rockets, who held the right of first refusal, meaning they had 15 days to either match the offer or work out compensation with us. We had intentionally inserted some clauses in the contract that would make it difficult for Houston to match.

There were clauses tied to attendance, clauses tied to endorsement opportunities, even clauses tied to others' accomplishments. Moses would be compensated, for instance, if none of his teammates made the All-Star team or finished among the league leaders in steals. Each was a virtual certainty in Philadelphia, since Doc was an All-Star fixture and Maurice was always among the top thieves. In Houston, the chances were much more remote.

When the Rockets raised objections, an arbitrator was called. He ruled some of the clauses illegal, but let others stand. Years later, John Nash didn't see much difference between those that were allowed, and those that weren't. And the clock continued to tick on Houston.

We talked compensation. They wanted center/forward Caldwell Jones and a 1983 first-round draft pick—a pick we had acquired from lowly Cleveland—for Malone.

Billy hated the idea of giving up Caldwell, a guy who cared little about individual accomplishments but would do anything to win. If that meant chasing Larry Bird around the perimeter, he would do it. If that meant banging with Kareem Abdul-Jabbar in the post, he would do that, too.

And, Billy said, "He was such a warrior. He'd play with a broken hand or nose. It didn't matter; he'd give it his best every night."

Nash remembers that Harold had less of a problem parting with C.J., because he had little interest in paying him starter's money to back up Moses. Harold claimed otherwise, saying in March 2007 that he too wanted to keep Caldwell. "But," he added, "Houston was adamant. We had no choice."

Billy reached the same conclusion, and said it was "narrow-minded" of him to want to hang on to Caldwell, despite his affection for the player. "The reality of pro sports," Billy said, "is that when you have an opportunity to get a talent like Moses, you do what you have to do."

But the way Del Harris remembers it, we really wouldn't have had to do anything. The Rockets' new owner, Charlie Thomas, had paid less than $10 million for the team. Now he was going to have to pay $13 million for his best player.

"He was appalled and shocked," Harris said. "He determined to let him go."

THE ONE THAT GOT AWAY

Caldwell, returning from a fishing trip at the Jersey Shore, stopped at a toll booth on the Atlantic City Expressway and he heard somebody yell, "Hey, Caldwell, we're sad to see you go."

"I didn't know what they were talking about," he recalled.

Once he made it home, he learned from his brothers that Billy had been trying to call him. He dialed his coach and learned what had happened.

"OK," he told Billy, "you guys can start planning the parade down Broad Street."

"A FORMALITY"

Bryan Abrams, a longtime season-ticket holder, immediately started thinking about a parade, too. He recalled that in previous years, there had been so many disappointments, so much heartache.

"You kept saying, 'This is our year, this is our year, this is our year'," he said. "When they sent Caldwell down to Houston and got Moses, it was our year. You absolutely knew as soon as Moses got there, it was over. It was done. As soon as we got him, it was, 'Start the parade.' I don't know why they bothered to play the season. It was a formality.

"That team, you knew from the start. You knew that sometime in June, you were going to go see a parade."

WELCOMING COMMITTEE

Tim Malloy, the Sixers' assistant group sales director, was the one who greeted Moses at the airport when he arrived in town. There was no great media scrum, no great fanfare, just Tim in his 1977 Toyota Corolla Hatchback, offering Moses a Shasta soda and a soft pretzel.

As it happened, the Phillies had a game against the Cardinals the night Moses arrived. And as Tim drove Moses through the crowded parking lot toward our offices in Veterans Stadium, the fans instantly recognized the large man crammed into the passenger's seat of Tim's car. They began pounding on the hood and cheering wildly. Moses was genuinely moved.

"In Houston, I could walk down the main street and no one would even look at me," he told Malloy. "Now look at this scene."

But his mood changed when he learned that we were giving up Caldwell to get him. He and C.J. had been teammates on the Spirit of St. Louis in the ABA and remained friends. Moses was, Katz remembered, "terribly upset" that they weren't going to be reunited, and balked at signing the contract. Harold pulled him aside, and told him he couldn't possibly back out now, after he had been given so much money—more than anyone else in the league. And not after the deal had already been announced.

"Please," Katz said, "just sign it." And Moses did.

Now it was time to meet the media, and Moses did so in a small room deep beneath the Vet's stands.

"Moses just be watchin'," he said in his typical shorthand. "It's still Doc's show."

2

Their deadline looming, reporters massed outside the visitors' locker room at the Los Angeles Forum late on the night of June 8, 1982.

It was a familiar vigil. The Sixers, eliminated by the Lakers in Game 6 of the Finals on this night, had also been championship-round losers in '77 and '80.

But those seeking fresh perspective would have to wait; the locker room remained closed to reporters beyond the usual ten-minute postgame cooling-off period.

Asked if the mob could be granted entry, Harold Katz shooed off first Harvey Pollack, then an NBA official.

It took some further coaxing, but finally the room was opened. The scene, recalled Don Benevento of the *Camden Courier-Post*, was unforgettable.

"Doc was crying," he said, referring to Julius Erving. "Bobby Jones was upset. Harold was upset."

While Benevento remembered the two veteran players being "pretty devastated," Bobby said he felt "disappointment," nothing more.

"At that point," he said, "my whole attitude was, if we win, great. If we lose, great. Either way, I get a vacation or a celebration."

Which is not to say Bobby didn't care; no one could ever properly make that claim of such a fierce competitor. It's just to say that he had a firm grasp of where basketball fit in the larger scheme of things.

Julius did, too. But this defeat hit him hard.

"I did cry," he remembered. It was the only time in his life he had done so after a basketball game, and the first time he had wept since losing his brother Marvin to lupus in 1969.

Erving, like many of his teammates, had been sure the Sixers were going to win this time. They were a better team than the Lakers, he believed. And the Sixers had the home-court advantage, not to mention momentum, having won an emotional Game 7 in Boston Garden to beat their hated rivals, the Celtics, in the Eastern Conference Finals.

The home-court advantage was short-lived, the Lakers winning Game 1 in the Spectrum and then holding serve.

"I felt the window of opportunity had closed in my career to win the NBA title," Doc said. "That was the third time we had come in second, and that's not the way you want the script to read."

SPARKLING LEGACY

Beloved by fans and respected by his peers, Julius Erving had transcended mere superstardom by this point. That was as much because of his uncommon decency as it was his greatness on the court.

"He was the classiest player I ever met," Pollack said. "In 50 years in the NBA, he was by far the classiest."

Another man who spent a half-century around Philadelphia sports, retired broadcaster Al Meltzer, echoed that, saying that Erving possessed "the perfect combination of talent and poise—a once-in-a-lifetime package."

"There is Dr. J, and there is only Dr. J," Meltzer said. "There is no No. 2."

Julius seemingly signed every autograph, did every interview, visited every hospital.

"Doc was more comfortable in his own skin than any other superstar I had seen up to that point," said Ray Didinger, then a columnist with the *Philadelphia Daily News* "He took the business of being an ambassador of basketball seriously."

"He would walk through a crowd of 1,000 people and make everybody feel he cared about them," said Mark McNamara, a rookie center on the championship team. "It was amazing."

I had seen that dozens of times, most vividly one summer at a basketball camp in Schroon Lake, New York. Doc flew all night from Denver, and despite sweltering heat, spent an entire day working with youngsters, offering encouragement and signing autographs. When I returned to my hotel room that night, I was moved to tears.

The more common reaction was shake-your-head amazement, as with a signature Julius moment recalled by Phil Jasner, who for years has covered the Sixers for the *Philadelphia Daily News*.

He and Erving had been first-class seatmates on a flight from San Antonio to Dallas, as Jasner did an interview for a long feature story. Upon landing they made their way to baggage claim, where dozens of high school cheerleaders, in town for a competition, had gathered.

Recognizing Erving immediately, they flocked to him, seeking an autograph. He said he would be happy to oblige, but only on one condition: They had to first perform their routines.

"For a second, they all blinked," Jasner said. "All of a sudden, I saw these kids in a huddle. And they were talking real quick. And they snapped out of it, and they began to do their routines."

A crowd formed. And when the girls had finished, Jasner said, "Julius sat down on a suitcase and said, 'Just be polite and get in line.' And he signed for every last one."

NAME RECOGNITION

It seemed Doc was that way every day. With his teammates. With the reporters who stood eight-deep around his locker following each game, win or lose. Even with opponents.

Billy McKinney, a rookie guard with the Kansas City-Omaha Kings in 1978-79, came out early for warm-ups before a game against the Sixers that first season. Erving was among the players loosening up at the far basket.

Doc took one last practice shot, then started off the court, in the direction of our locker room. Then he did a quick about-face and walked over to McKinney.

"Billy," he said, "welcome to the league."

"I couldn't believe it—Dr. J knew who I was," McKinney remembered. "After the game, I called everyone I knew to tell them what happened: Dr. J knew my name."

It was the same for Utah Jazz center Mark Eaton, who began an 11-year pro career in 1982-83. Julius, he said, possessed a "statesman-like demeanor," and was "the ultimate gentleman."

"As a young player," Eaton said, "he'd go out of his way to talk to me."

Then the game would start, and as the 7-foot-5 Eaton recalled, Julius would "go out and dunk on my head."

PERFECT TEAMMATE

Within the confines of our locker room, Julius was seen as "a great player, but an even better teammate," according to Mike Dunleavy, a rookie guard in 1976-77. Everyone was accorded respect, no matter where they stood in the pecking order. He would mingle with the frontline guys, but also reach out to those who seldom played; Jim Spanarkel, a deep reserve with us in '79-80, recalled that Doc always treated him "like a starter."

When Andrew Toney didn't have anywhere to go for Thanksgiving or Christmas dinner his first year in town ('80-81), Doc invited him over to the Erving home on the Main Line. When Marc Iavaroni didn't have a place to stay his rookie season ('82-83), Doc told him he was welcome to use the Ervings' spare bedroom; Marc wound up living there for a month.

"I was really good friends with him," said Henry Bibby, a guard who was Doc's Sixers teammate from '76-77 through '79-80. "He was just always there. It wasn't one thing with Julius; it was everything with him. One of the nicest people you could ever meet. One of the nicest superstars you could ever meet. . . . Just a genuine person."

Another friend was veteran forward Steve Mix, who kicked off their relationship by taping Doc's Converse high-tops together and throwing them atop the locker-room lights before Julius debuted with us, in an October 1976 game against San Antonio in the Spectrum.

It was an odd pairing. Julius was a star, while Mix was a journeyman, a guy who had been cut six times—once by the '72-73 Sixers, whose 9-73 record remains the worst in NBA history.

Mix finally stuck in '73-74, and a year later he was an All-Star. The fans took to him because he played hard and could shoot, most often from a spot on the baseline that came to be known as "Mixville."

Erving's arrival meant that Mixville had a new tenant. Mix knew the score, knew his minutes were about to take a hit. (He would, in fact, play over 1,000 fewer in '76-77 than he did the year before.) There was nothing to be gained by being bitter, by not trying to get along.

Julius Erving, "The Babe Ruth of Basketball," denies Phoenix Suns forward Jeff Cook at the rim. *Philadelphia Daily News/Michael Mercanti*

Hence the shoes-atop-the-lights welcome.

It was generally agreed that the friendship benefited both men. The ultra-serious Erving straightened Mix out, while the happy-go-lucky Mix loosened Erving up.

Then again, maybe it was more the latter than the former.

The Sixers were in Milwaukee the night Georgetown met North Carolina for the 1982 NCAA men's basketball championship. Doc invited Mix and *Inquirer* beat writer George Shirk to his hotel room to watch the game, and beforehand they ordered hot-fudge sundaes from room service.

The first half unfolded. No sundaes.

Halftime arrived. Still nothing.

At that point Erving rose to use the bathroom, and Mix sprang into action, phoning room service and in his best Doc voice asking, in no uncertain terms, just where in creation the blasted hot-fudge sundaes might be. Or words to that effect.

They arrived in an instant.

"He doesn't need to know about this," Mix whispered to Shirk.

CLASS FOR ALL OCCASIONS

Obliged under the terms of his contract to make four appearances on behalf of the team each year, Doc routinely made 200 or more. He gave of his time to such charities as the Special Olympics, March of Dimes, Lupus Foundation, American Dental Association, Police Athletic League, Hemophilia Foundation, and Pennsylvania Adult Education.

He reached out in unexpected ways, too. One time Fred Liedman, our director of advertising sales, was looking to close a big deal. Doc offered to help, inviting the clients, who happened to be Jewish, to his home for dinner—a Friday night Shabbat dinner.

And as Liedman recalled, the meal served by Doc and his wife Turquoise included "brisket, kugel, kasha with bow ties."

"Amazing," Fred said. "We signed the deal right in their home. Could you imagine that happening in today's NBA?"

Matt Guokas Jr. was likewise amazed the first time he crossed paths with Doc. Matty's first year as a radio analyst was also Doc's first year in town (1976-77), and Guokas looked for an opportunity to introduce himself.

It came on a flight out of Kansas City, after a loss to the Kings in which

Erving had played poorly. Finding an empty seat next to Doc (who, Matty remembered, was paying his bills), Guokas sat down. Julius put his checkbook aside and they settled into a conversation, Doc somehow remembering that his Nets faced the Bulls, for whom Matty had played guard, in an exhibition a few years earlier.

"What impressed me so much was how poised and professional he was, where most players would be mad," said Guokas, who would become an assistant coach on the championship team (and, a few years later, the head coach). "He acted the same way as if he'd scored 35 points. He had the ability to keep himself under control and be nice to people. That stuck with me the whole 11 years."

It was the same with reporters. Julius gave generously of his time to every one of them—"from the *New York Times* to the local high school [paper]," Billy Cunningham said.

Because Doc stayed so long at his locker after games, we stopped using a team bus on the road and instead rented a fleet of luxury cars. That way his teammates could head off into the night, and Julius could satisfy the cameras and the notepads.

And when even more was asked, he willingly complied. During the '82-83 season, a writer for the *Seattle Times* named Steve Kelley came to a game in Portland and asked Doc about doing an interview. Julius told him to stop by his hotel room in Seattle the following day, and Steve did so, sitting and talking for two hours.

"You can't do that today," Kelley said, sounding much like Fred Liedman. "Can you imagine spending two hours in Shaq or Kobe's room? No way that would happen."

ROLE MODEL TO THE STARS

When I accompanied Julius and some other NBA players to China in the summer of 1982, our itinerary included a stop in the city of Xian. We were lodged out in the country, in the Xian version of a Holiday Inn. Julius and his wife, Turquoise, were assigned the only nice room in the whole place, and at our meeting that night he said he felt guilty about it, that he wanted to move.

San Antonio Spurs forward Gene Banks, who grew up in Philadelphia idolizing Doc, immediately spoke up.

"Doc, you do deserve it," he said, "because of the example you set for all of us. Enjoy it, and stop worrying."

Doc's example was not lost on the stars who followed him into the NBA.

"Magic Johnson and Michael Jordan always pointed that out," said *Sports Illustrated*'s Jack McCallum. "He had a dignity about him that spread throughout the league. He was a huge part of how people acted around the league."

The other part of his legacy, McCallum said, is the way he "legitimized street." Blessed with immense hands, the hangtime of a pterodactyl, and the desire to try anything, he took showmanship beyond that of Connie Hawkins and Elgin Baylor. He took it to new heights—literally.

"Doc put the game above the rim, and it's never come down," said broadcaster Al Meltzer. "But with him, it wasn't a show. That's just the way he did his job."

Darrell Griffith was among those who followed in his footsteps, a skywalker who starred for the University of Louisville's "Doctors of Dunk" and later enjoyed a long NBA career.

"As a fellow dunker," Griffith recalled, "Doc was the measuring stick."

A Louisville company decided early in Griffith's college career that he measured up, coming out with a poster that showed him throwing one down alongside the words, "Move over, Dr. J." It was, Griffith remembered, "the ultimate compliment."

Any Erving highlight montage invariably includes grainy video from a slam-dunk competition at the 1976 ABA All-Star Game in Denver, when he took off from just inside the foul line and slammed. And it includes his baseline move in Game 4 of the 1980 Finals against the Lakers, when he took off on the right side of the lane, soared past an earthbound forward named Mark Landsberger, and, waving the ball in one giant paw, floated past Kareem Abdul-Jabbar and laid it up on the other side of the glass.

That one left everyone agape, especially Magic Johnson. He would later tell reporters that he didn't know whether to take the ball out, or ask Doc to do it again.

Abdul-Jabbar seemed less impressed: "That shot was the one that got through out of the many that he attempted," he said in March 2007. "His perseverance was the part of him that enabled him to finally make that shot."

LICENSE TO FLY

Growing up on Long Island, Julius offered only hints of the type of player he would become. While he starred in high school, other players—kids like Tom Riker and Bill Chamberlain—were more highly regarded. So as Riker headed off to South Carolina (and later to the New York Knicks) and Chamberlain set out for North Carolina, Erving settled for Massachusetts of the low-profile Yankee Conference.

These were the days before ESPN, and before freshman eligibility. The no-dunk rule was still in effect.

But word began to leak out about the new kid with the huge hands who could, well, fly. He led the freshman team to an undefeated season even though he was shaken by his brother Marvin's death from lupus, a disease of the body's connective tissue that imitates other diseases, like a heart attack or even a brain tumor.

Julius cried for three days, then stopped. He would often recall it as a key moment in his life. Before that, he felt such power and control; basketball, he said, gave him "a license to fly." But Marvin's death made Julius realize how fleeting that gift was.

"I felt hopeless," he said, "but I also became fearless." His motto became, "Dare to be great."

"It means," he said years later, "your boundaries are limitless in life."

By this point he was 6-foot-7, some three and a half inches taller than he had been when he began college, and he was toying with opponents. He averaged 26 points a game as a sophomore, 27 as a junior, and had made UMass games such an event that students stood in line for hours, waiting for the gates to the venerable Curry Hicks Cage to open; the school's cafeteria took to dispensing box lunches that came to be known as "Cage Survival Kits."

Pro scouts began to notice him, if only in a roundabout way. The Cincinnati Royals were amid an East Coast swing when their general manager, Joe Axelson, asked coach Bob Cousy, the former Celtics star, to take a look at a guard for Manhattan. Manhattan happened to be hosting UMass. After the game, Cousy called Axelson.

"The Manhattan kid can't play, but I just saw the best college player in history," Cousy said. "He's Julius Erving, a junior. He can do absolutely anything he wants to do. He's Connie Hawkins, but he can put the ball on the floor with anybody."

Julius had outgrown the Yankee Conference. Moreover, his mother was ill, and he felt it was his responsibility to support her. So he began testing the professional waters. The stodgy old NBA had rules prohibiting its teams from drafting underclassmen. But the upstart ABA had no such restrictions, and indeed was always looking for ways to beat the established league to talented players.

The New York Nets owned his rights, but the Virginia Squires bought out the Nets, then hammered out a contract in an all-night bargaining session in a hotel near the Philadelphia airport.

Very early in a tryout camp, the Squires discovered how good Erving was: so good that they sent him home, fearing he might be injured; so good that they traded one of their starting forwards, George Carter; so good that a nickname was born.

A classmate back on Long Island, Leon Saunders, had taken to calling Erving "The Doctor" after Julius had labeled him "The Professor" for his classroom acumen. Squires teammate Willie Sojourner took it one step further, dubbing him "Dr. J" because of his acrobatic moves.

If Erving was great during his two years in Virginia, he was even better when he wound up back with the Nets, winning or sharing three ABA MVP awards in as many seasons, and capturing a pair of championships. It is often said that if you didn't see Doc then—soaring through the air, holding that red, white and blue ball in one huge paw, his Afro flopping in the breeze—you never really saw him at all.

Which means few really did.

Hubie Brown, who coached the Kentucky Colonels in that league, would not argue that point, saying that Doc did things in the ABA that were "absolutely eye-opening."

Like swoop downcourt on a fast break, catch a pass, soar through the lane, tap the top of the box on the backboard—11 feet above the floor—and dunk.

"He would do it religiously," said Brown, who would coach the Hawks, Knicks, and Grizzlies later in his Hall of Fame career before becoming a respected broadcaster.

And because of stuff like that, Hubie said, "He would turn your building against you. If you let him come down on the three-lane break and take off at the foul line and dunk, people in your own building would give him a standing ovation."

Tired of it, Brown began fining his players $50 in 1975-76, if they did not foul Erving in the open court, long before he reached the lane.

"Fifty dollars back then was a lot of money," Hubie said. But none of the Colonels ever cheapshotted Doc. Nobody did.

"That was the respect for him," Brown said. "Plus everybody understood what he meant to the league. And he was such a good person, on and off the court. Even the wildest player in the league had the utmost respect for Julius. Nobody would deliberately hit him in the air.

"He was your spokesman, and thank God he was your spokesman."

"THE BABE RUTH OF BASKETBALL"

The ABA died after the '75-76 season, but the NBA agreed to accept four teams. The entry fee would be steep, however—$3.2 million per club, due by September 15, 1976. Nets owner Roy Boe didn't have that kind of cash, and Erving was now claiming that the team had promised to renegotiate his contract if the leagues ever merged.

Boe did not believe any such promise had been made, but he had no choice: He began shopping Dr. J around. The Knicks turned him down, but I had put in a call to Nets general manager Billy Melchionni, a former Sixers guard, telling him to keep us in mind if they couldn't patch things up with Doc.

Billy had called, so I drove out to the estate of Fitz Dixon, our new owner.

"Fitz, there is a player available from the other league," I said, pausing for effect. "And his name is Julius Erving."

Silence. Fitz knew horses, not hoops. He finally asked, "Now tell me, who is he?"

"Uh, well, he's kind of the Babe Ruth of basketball," I said.

I told Fitz more. He grew interested. Finally he asked just what it was the Nets wanted in return for this Julius Erving. I held my breath and told Fitz: $3 million. Then I told him it would take another $3 million to sign Julius.

"Are you recommending this?" he asked.

"Yes sir, I am."

"Fine and dandy, then. Let's do it," he said.

Next I had to sell our coach, Gene Shue, as well as our cornerstone, George McGinnis, on the idea.

I called Gene, and we talked for a while. Finally I played my trump card.

Knowing that the Knicks were interested in Doc, and knowing Gene's distaste for that particular franchise (born of repeated playoff failures against New York while he coached the Baltimore Bullets), I posed a question: "Gene, if you picked up the paper tomorrow morning and read the headline, 'New York Knicks acquire Julius Erving,' how would you feel?"

That was enough. "Oh, get it done," Gene said.

I told George McGinnis what was in the works after a preseason doubleheader in Madison Square Garden. But I also told him I wouldn't proceed without his blessing. He gave it, but in retrospect I'm not sure I gave him much choice.

On October 21, we finalized the deal for Julius, sending $3 million to the Nets and signing him for $450,000 a year over the next six years.

Julius Erving had become the $6 Million Man.

"Julius, where do you bank?" a reporter asked him at his introductory news conference.

"I think that's an unfair question," Doc said. It was one of the few times during his 11 years in Philadelphia that Julius directed anything resembling a cross word in the direction of a reporter. No one has ever treated the city's often-prickly media corps so respectfully, and he was beloved for that.

NOTHIN' BUT A HEARTACHE

When we met Portland in the 1977 Finals at the end of Doc's first season, it was billed as playground versus purity, a battle between the undisciplined Sixers and the unselfish Blazers, led by coach Jack Ramsay and their ponytailed center Bill Walton.

Playground prevailed early on; we won the first two games. But the Blazers ultimately took the series in six.

Julius had been everything we might have hoped for, on the court and off it. But in the off-season we asked something more from him: Would he take part in our new ad campaign?

He agreed. In time our fans saw the following on their television screens: Doc closing a locker, turning toward the camera, raising an elongated index finger and saying, "We owe you one."

If nothing else, it was memorable.

EXTREME MAKEOVER

The Sixers did not reach the Finals in '78 or '79—We Owe You Three?—and when we returned in 1980, things were vastly different than they had been three years earlier. Billy Cunningham, once a star player, was now the coach, and the roster had been reshaped.

George McGinnis was gone, as were guys like World B. Free and Joe Bryant. In their places were players like Maurice Cheeks, Lionel Hollins, and Bobby Jones. It was now Doc's team. And as Billy noted, "[He] wanted the responsibility."

But the end result wasn't much different, even though Kareem Abdul-Jabbar badly sprained an ankle in the fifth game of the Finals, which the Lakers won to take a 3-2 lead.

The two teams flew East. Abdul-Jabbar stayed behind.

"I'd be lying if I said our confidence didn't jump a notch or two upon hearing Kareem was out," Julius wrote in a first-person story that appeared in the *Wall Street Journal* in June 2005.

When Game 6 began, rookie point guard Magic Johnson stood in against Caldwell Jones for the opening tip, which C.J., by the way, won.

But that, Caldwell recalled, "was about the only thing we got that night."

What followed was the first signature moment of Magic's pro career, a 42-point, 15-rebound, seven-assist masterpiece that earned him the first of five championship rings.

Even Abdul-Jabbar, watching on television in the bedroom of his Los Angeles home, said he was "amazed" at what he saw.

"Once the tone was set," he said in March 2007, "the 76ers were unable to figure out how to get over the hump." That was a recurring problem.

AVERTING DISASTER

The following year the Sixers needed to win one of the last three games against the Celtics in the Eastern Conference finals to advance to the championship round, in which Houston—a team that had Moses Malone and little else—would be the opponent.

We lost all three, by a total of five points. And Boston did indeed beat the Rockets for the title.

The year after that, we again led the Celtics 3-1 in the Eastern Finals. And again we lost Game 5. And Game 6.

The decisive game would be played in Boston Garden.

"There is a word for the Sixers' situation," *Inquirer* columnist Bill Lyon wrote. "Hopeless."

Others weren't so sure. St. Joseph University women's coach Jim Foster watched the Sixers practice the day before Game 7 in the school's fieldhouse, and sensed confidence, not dread.

"I knew they'd win at Boston," he said.

The game would be played on a Sunday afternoon. As the team rode the bus from a hotel in Cambridge to Boston that morning, George Shirk, the *Inquirer* beat guy, listened as Erving talked to his teammates about the places they could visit in Los Angeles during the Finals. It was a transparent ploy, Shirk thought. No way do they win this game.

During warm-ups a few enterprising Boston fans swooped past the Sixers bench, wearing bed sheets that had "Ghosts of Celtics past" scrawled on the front.

"That's when I got worried," Erving later told reporters. "I thought it was the Klan."

Cunningham was in a foul mood, angry at the fans and at the press. He pulled his players off the court before the game and urged them to win it for themselves.

Shockingly, they did. Erving scored 29 points (20 in the second half), in what Shirk would later call "the quintessential Erving game." But it was just as much the quintessential Andrew Toney game. The daring young guard scored 34 against M.L. Carr and the conga line of defenders that followed.

It wasn't the first time Toney had lit up the Celtics, and it wouldn't be the last; he came to be known as "The Boston Strangler."

Our players had a nickname for Carr, too: "Lunchbox." That's because Toney so often ate his lunch.

As the clock wound down on our 120-106 rout, Celtics fans began chanting, "Beat L-A, Beat L-A." And while the players celebrated, Cunningham fumed. Lyon swears that the coach spent an entire late-game timeout staring him down.

Billy's mood had not improved when he met reporters afterward.

"I'm going to be real quick," he began. "I only have two things to say. No. 1, I want to thank the Celtics' fans for the way they responded at the end, because that showed real class.

"No. 2, I'm ecstatic for the 12 guys and the coaches, and that's it. Everyone else buried us. Period. Good-bye. That's it for me, babe. I've had enough of you guys."

The players didn't share his view. "This feels too good to be bitter," Cheeks told reporters.

Harold Katz took a pragmatic viewpoint. "If we had lost, this franchise would have been very, very shaky," he told reporters. "We would have lost the confidence of an entire city. We probably wouldn't have sold only a handful of season tickets. Now this team should be all-time heroes. This is probably the greatest feeling I've had in my entire life."

Cunningham sat off to the side, puffing on a cigar. He waved off a camera crew. He couldn't be bothered.

Lyon swallowed hard, then tiptoed over. "The line for apologies forms here," he said, extending his hand and using a line that would serve as the lead for his column the following day.

For a moment Lyon thought Cunningham might hit him. He did not.

"That hurt a lot," Billy said, referring to Lyon's pregame column.

"It was supposed to," Lyon said. But as Lyon recalled years later, "No grudge was held. I give him all the credit in the world for that."

The Finals only brought more pain. Which is why Dr. J wept. And why Harold Katz, in the meantime, schemed.

3

For Harold Katz, the last straw had come on a Sunday afternoon in April 1982. He had seen Boston manhandle the Sixers in the Spectrum. He had watched as the Celtics dominated the backboards while wiping out a 13-point halftime deficit en route to an overtime victory. And he was fuming.

It was one thing to witness a collapse like that from his seat at midcourt, as he had in his eight years as a season-ticket holder. It was quite another when you owned the team.

The South Philly native had bought the Sixers from Fitz Dixon in July 1981, having made his millions in the weight-loss business. From the very beginning he'd made it clear he would be a hands-on owner.

"The main problem with the 76ers was the lack of someone at the helm, a lack of direction," Katz told *Philadelphia Magazine* in November 1981. "Dixon ran it as a hobby, and he had very little involvement with the team. I don't think sports should be treated as a hobby. It's a business, and I intend to run it as I run my other businesses."

He also told the magazine that while the team had the right coach in Billy Cunningham and the right players, there "was something lacking to make them win that final game."

"Maybe," Harold added, "it's motivation. Maybe it's luck. Whatever it is, I'm gonna supply it."

CHOCOLATE THUNDER FLYIN'. . . OCCASIONALLY

The source of Harold's frustration that April day (as on many days that first season) was Darryl Dawkins. Drafted out of Maynard Evans High School in Orlando, Florida, seven years earlier, he remained something of a riddle. He was big, but he didn't always play big. He was skilled, but also maddeningly inconsistent.

Even so, his teammates loved him, and his shtick played well with the media. He referred to himself as "Chocolate Thunder," and said he hailed from the planet Lovetron. He also nicknamed his dunks, most notably one of his two backboard-breaking slams during the 1979-80 season, which came against the Kansas City Kings and a forward named Bill Robinzine. That one, Darryl said, was the "Chocolate Thunder Flyin', Robinzine Cryin', Teeth Shakin', Glass Breakin', Rump Roastin', Bun Toastin', Wham, Bam, I Am Jam."

Nor did Darryl confine his glass-breakin' and teeth-shakin' to game night. One time Billy Cunningham, upset at a bad road loss, convened a practice at some out-of-the-way gym in Philadelphia.

"I told everyone if I broke a backboard, we'd be out of practice," Dawkins remembered in February 2006.

One rim looked particularly vulnerable. "About two minutes later," Darryl said, "it went boom."

With predictable results. "Billy went berserk," recalled guard Clint Richardson.

"He said, 'Darryl, you're paying for that,'" Dawkins said. "So he turned us sideways to play on the wooden baskets. Finally he said, 'Get out of the gym.'"

TIME FOR A CHANGE

Billy would pull Darryl aside and try to tell him he needed to be more serious about the game. After doing so on one occasion, Darryl tripped his coach as he walked away.

Assistant coaches Jack McMahon and Chuck Daly offered their own tutorials, but nothing helped. Dawkins, though 6-foot-11 and heavily muscled, wasn't always interested in mixing it up underneath; one year Denver guard T.R. Dunn collected more rebounds than he did. Darryl's defense was similarly spotty; he routinely led the team in fouls and disqualifications.

His health was also an issue in '81-82; he broke a bone in his leg and missed 26 games, finally returning in April. But his fourth game back was the one against Boston, in which he shot 1-for-7 and stood idly by as the Celtics paraded to the glass.

All of this was going through Harold Katz's mind as he marched from his luxury box to the locker room. He huddled with Billy Cunningham, then met the press.

"Our guys are too nice," he began. "Check it out. Our team leads the league in picking guys up off the floor." He promised changes if the team didn't win a championship—"serious changes."

"I don't know if that would mean one change, two changes, or five changes, but I know there'd be some. It's apparent that we have a rebounding problem. How do you win a championship the way we rebound?"

A few years earlier, we had been criticized for being undisciplined, for being a disconnected bunch of me-firsters. We had reshaped the roster, rebuilt the team—rebuilt it as a cohesive, unselfish, defensive-minded group. But now we were too nice.

Harold met with Darryl the next day, and though there were some bright spots in the playoffs—as when Darryl scored 27 points and blocked eight shots in the opener of a first-round series against Atlanta—little changed. By the time we lost in the Finals to the Lakers, Harold knew we needed to find a new center.

A FRESH START

The trade finally came on August 27, while I was on that trip to the Far East: Darryl to the Nets for a 1983 first-round pick and $700,000.

Looking back over two decades after the fact, Dawkins said, "Yeah, I needed to get a fresh start—go somewhere where I could play, and continue to learn more about the game. It was like getting a fresh start, because I did not like Harold Katz, he did not like me, and he was my boss."

Darryl didn't stop there: "Katz is one of the guys that made me not want to play basketball anymore. Harold Katz [honked] me off so bad, if I was at his funeral, I probably would have pushed his casket over. He made the game not fun."

Darryl would exact his revenge two years later.

"FUELER BLUSH"

The wave of feature stories that heralded Harold's arrival as an NBA owner invariably noted that he played point guard on an Olney High team that faced Wilt Chamberlain's powerful Overbrook High club in 1952. And lost, 80-22.

Also mentioned was the fact that Harold's dad died the year he graduated from high school, leaving him to operate the family grocery store, Kettyle's Market, at the corner of Chew and Wister in the city's Germantown section. Harold hated it. He was 18; while he was working long hours, his friends were all going down to the Jersey Shore every weekend, partying and chasing girls.

He stuck with it for a few years, then married and got into sales, first with Fuller Brush. It was an odd career choice considering he had a stuttering problem, but he would later say he viewed it as therapeutic, as a way to cure his impediment.

Early on, he told *Philadelphia Magazine*, he was paired with a veteran salesman who had a lisp. First house they went to, they knocked on the door. No answer. The graybeard, eager to impress the rookie with his persistence, kept knocking. And knocking. Finally a housewife stuck her head out of a second-floor window.

"Who the hell are you?"

"Ful-Ful-Ful," Katz stammered.

"Fueler Blush," the other guy said. "Fueler Blush."

She came downstairs and opened the door for these two strange creatures. They gave their pitch, and, as the story goes, wound up making a sale— "a sympathy sale," Harold told the *Boston Globe*.

There were other sales jobs, and Harold finally turned his attention to franchising. Most of the franchising in the country at that time was concentrated in two areas—food and auto parts—and he had no interest in either. But one day he was talking to his mother about her weight problem. He asked her how much she spent each week on diet pills, trips to the spa, and whatnot. She thought it might be as much as $60.

A light bulb went off. Weight Watchers was the only nationwide weight-control chain, so Harold decided to make a go of it as well. He founded Shape Up Weight Control in 1971, opening a single center in the suburb of Willow Grove. Another soon opened in Ardmore.

By 1976, at age 38, he was a millionaire. Five years later, his net worth was said to be $300 million, and his weight-loss empire, now called Nutri/Systems, had expanded to over 500 centers nationwide.

ONCE A POINT GUARD, ALWAYS A POINT GUARD

Basketball was still in Harold's blood. He had approached Fitz Dixon about buying the Sixers in 1979, but had gotten no response. Next he explored the possibility of acquiring an expansion franchise.

Harold paid a visit to St. Louis, which along with Dallas was being considered for a team. He was accompanied by David Stern, then the league's deputy commissioner under Larry O'Brien, as well as another league official, Joe Axelson.

Axelson was struck by Harold's energy and passion. "He was so full of basketball history, ideas and opinions—on everything from ticket costs to the abilities of the league's sixth men," Axelson recalled. "Interesting guy."

The league ultimately decided to expand to Dallas, not St. Louis, so Harold was left to seek other options. He considered buying the Clippers when they came on the market in 1980. He looked into buying the Phillies in the spring of '81 but dropped out, he later told the *New York Times*, when a bidding war broke out.

"I don't get involved in bidding wars," he told them.

Finally Fitz went public with his frustrations over our playoff failures and flagging attendance. We had drawn just 11,448 fans per home date in 1980-81, nearly 7,000 under capacity, despite winning 62 games. Even more troubling was the fact that we attracted 7,208 for a playoff game against Indiana, and 6,704 for a Game 7 against Milwaukee.

Hearing Dixon's discontent, Harold pounced. He was at the forefront of negotiations—negotiations that Fitz left to his attorneys—agreeing after six weeks of talks to buy the team on July 9, 1981, for a little over $12 million.

"Since I can't play for the Sixers and I can't coach them," he said at his introductory news conference, "the second-best thing is to own them."

He also said this: "I've seen the craziness that's going on in pro sports, and I guarantee you I won't contribute to it. I will not be the type of owner who pays ridiculous salaries to mediocre talent."

Moses Malone-type talent would prove to be another matter. But first he set out to cut expenses and increase attendance. He took the team's travel arrangements away from the agency owned by Billy Cunningham.

"Pure economics," he told the *Boston Globe*. "No knock on Billy."

Harold also confiscated the credit cards Fitz had given the assistant coaches and trainer, for entertaining and dining on the road. That, Katz told the *Globe*, would save $100,000 a year.

The cheerleaders? History. That would save another $55,000.

The pregame spread in the pressroom? Let them eat bag lunches. That would save another $60,000, according to the *Globe* piece.

Harold also had some ideas about how to pique the fans' interest. As his first season wore on, he wooed Wilt, his old high school nemesis. Didn't matter that Chamberlain, by then 45, had retired in 1973. He still played volleyball, still kept himself in remarkable shape. Presumably he would be capable of giving us a jolt on the floor and, just as importantly, the gate.

Wilt ultimately informed Harold—via telegram—that he wasn't interested in March 1982. If we were going to find a new center, we would have to look elsewhere.

4

Billy Cunningham loved coaching, but hated what it did to him. He hated the fact that he was always preoccupied with the next game, the next season. He hated that he could never fully celebrate the victories, while the losses always lingered.

"The game," he said, "was always there."

He couldn't sleep on the road, couldn't focus on what was important at home: "I knew I was not as good a husband and father as I should've been," he said. He knew he "needed to be there" for his wife, Sondra, and daughters Stephanie and Heather.

Now, in his sixth season as coach, he had his best team. There were no excuses for falling short this time. The burden upon him was, in the estimation of former *Daily News* columnist Mark Whicker, "immense."

"If he had any fun during those years, he kept it to himself," Whicker, now with the *Orange County Register*, recalled. "He was a different person than he had been previously, and he got a little more uptight each year." And, Whicker believed, "more obsessed with winning."

"The whole grind aged him and his personality changed," he said, "but in 1982-83, Billy's will drove that team to the title."

George Shirk, then the *Inquirer* beat writer, compared Billy to Ahab. Seldom had he seen someone so driven.

"He was a wreck," Shirk said. "I didn't even know him at the end. I don't think he even knew himself."

Billy did not disagree. "I probably pushed very hard that year," he said.

"[The players] knew it, and they wanted the same thing I wanted. . . . I wasn't going to allow them to become complacent, no matter what happened. We just pushed and pushed and pushed them."

CONSTANT INTERACTION

It's not like Billy had been a pushover before that 1982-83 season.

"He was the toughest coach I ever played for—by far," said Franklin Edwards, a reserve guard on the title team. "And he was the best coach I ever played for."

Billy sought perfection, nothing less. He was, Clint Richardson said, "anal about execution," and when he didn't get the desired results, was apt to explode, or worse. After particularly galling road losses, he sometimes took the team straight from the airport to the practice court; the players took to calling such sessions "Bataan Death Marches."

Caldwell Jones believed Billy, once a Hall of Fame forward for the Sixers, simply took the same approach to coaching that he had to playing, that it wasn't a matter of him being a perfectionist so much as a competitor. Billy, it often seemed, played every game from the sideline, whistling and stomping and gesturing and agonizing—not to mention officiating.

"As referees, we understood Billy Cunningham's tenacity," retired referee Ed T. Rush said. "We knew we'd have interaction with him during the evening."

His players did, too.

"He's a great guy," former Sixers guard Lionel Hollins said. "I love Billy. During a game he would go ballistic. He would [tick] you off most of the time. But afterward it was, 'Way to go, babe.' He was a good guy. I liked playing for him."

So too did Darryl Dawkins.

"He could [honk] you off, but he'd [honk] you off because he was a competitor," Darryl said. "He wanted to win everything."

Jack McCaffery, who worked for the *Trenton Times* then and is now a columnist for the *Delaware County Daily Times*, thought Billy coached the Sixers as if they were a college team. Instead of acknowledging that there would be lulls in performance brought on by the grind of the 82-game season, he sought the sort of excellence a Top-25 college club is more likely to achieve over the course of 30 games or so.

To Billy, McCaffery believed, "Every game meant something."

EMOTIONAL RESCUE

If Billy would detonate at the drop of a hat early in his coaching career, by 1982-83 his outbursts were more calculated, more of a means to an end.

"Sometimes," Billy said, "you want your team to be upset with you. . . . You get to the point where you have an idea of what buttons to push."

He cared not a bit if the players were ticked at him. The way he looked at it, at least that meant they were united about something.

Which is not to say that every outburst was a means to an end.

"When he got angry, he got that crazed look on his face, and he stared at you," said John Nash, our assistant general manager that year. "You didn't quite know what he was going to do. And he was a big enough man [at 6-foot-7 and well over 200 pounds], that for a short period of time he could have held his own with anybody, including the big guys. I think everybody was a little bit intimidated by Billy, and he used that to his advantage."

Intimidated? Clint Richardson said he was "terrified" of Billy: "No way was I going to rebel against him," Clint said, "I had such high respect for him."

Richardson swore that after a loss, Cunningham would sit in the front seat of the team bus and bury his face in a newspaper. And then, Clint said, "He wouldn't talk to us for days. If we lost two games in a row, it was death."

After a victory, Clint claimed, Billy would ditch the newspaper. If he were really in a good mood (and the team was on the road), he might join the rest of the staff—Nash, assistants Matt Guokas Jr. and Jack McMahon, trainer Al Domenico, and broadcaster Neil Funk—for a game of Liars Poker.

But for the most part he brooded. As the season (and in particular, the postseason) wore on, he dropped weight. The color drained from his face.

"I don't think he was tormented so much as he was competitive," Funk said. "He knew he had a team that should win it and could win it. That's pressure, because people are expecting you to be good."

THE KANGAROO KID

Billy Cunningham had been a star, the sixth man on the Sixers' great 1966-67 championship team, and ultimately a Hall of Famer. Nicknamed the "Kangaroo Kid" because of his jumping ability, he played with uncommon ferocity, his game having been honed on the playgrounds of Brooklyn and refined at North Carolina, under a young coach named Dean Smith.

But Billy's playing career, like his coaching career, would have its share of frustrations. In 1967-68 he broke his wrist during the Eastern Conference Finals against Boston, a big reason the Celtics came back from a 3-1 deficit to win the best-of-seven series.

He never sniffed a title as a player after '66-67, and his career ended, for all intents and purposes, on December 5, 1975.

Attempting a crossover move in the open court against the Knicks' Butch Beard, he crumpled to the floor, his shrieks of pain echoing throughout the Spectrum. His left knee was shredded.

A comeback attempt proved fruitless, and when he announced his retirement in October 1976, the *Daily News'* Phil Jasner began his story this way: "I was in the Spectrum on December 5, 1975, and sometimes I wish I could forget. But I cannot."

I can't, either. The emotion that night was overwhelming, but it didn't really hit me until the next morning, a Saturday. I took my family to a pancake house near our home in Moorestown, New Jersey, and as we entered the place I saw the front page of the *Philadelphia Inquirer* in a newspaper box.

Above the fold was a huge picture of Billy writhing on the floor, holding his knee, screaming out in agony. I broke down.

Billy settled into private business, and gave little thought to coaching. That changed when I called him late on the night of November 2, 1977.

The Sixers had just lost to Chicago to fall to 2-4. Fitz Dixon was at odds with our coach, Gene Shue. Change was in the air.

The more we talked, the more interested Billy became. He would later tell the *New York Times* that he knew he had to give it a shot, that he missed the game much more than he realized.

We finalized a contract and introduced him as our coach on the morning of November 4, nine hours before we were to play the Nets at Rutgers University's fieldhouse.

That first night, he sweat so much that his blue shirt could have been put through a wringer. Coincidence or not, we scored the game's last ten points and won by three.

DEFENSIVE-MINDED

Billy was intent on solidifying the defense, which he believed had gone soft under Shue. It was at that end of the floor, Billy believed, that a team

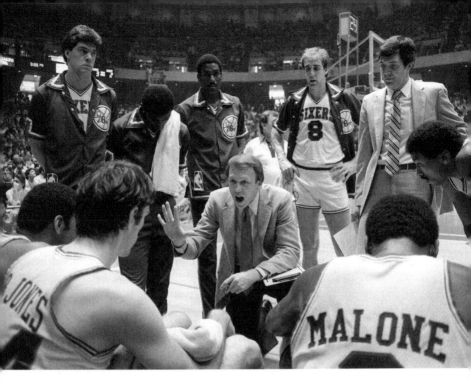

Billy Cunningham, always hard-driving, instructs the team during a timeout in a playoff game against Milwaukee. *Philadelphia Daily News/Michael Mercanti*

developed unity and pride. That he arrived at that conclusion was something of a surprise, because Billy, while a prolific scorer and rebounder as a player, had little interest in guarding anybody.

"I'd have had issues with me as a player if I'd been coaching [myself]," Billy admitted.

He was just as aware of his shortcomings as a coach. When he took the job, he later told the *New York Times*, "I was weak in the Xs and Os department. I [had] never had to explain anything in basketball terms, nor did I have any idea what to expect. I wasn't even a good practice player, especially when things were going well for us."

We had retained assistant coach Jack McMahon, and we added former Penn coach Chuck Daly once we met Chuck's asking price of a $35,000 yearly salary. Chuck would teach Billy how to organize practices. Jack, who had been around forever, would teach Billy and Chuck the league.

Billy often said that having two coaches of that caliber at his side was the best thing that ever happened to him. "They had a great impact," he said.

Daly told him over a bottle of wine that he had to assert himself, that he had to put his imprint on the team. Another time, when the team was struggling, Billy met individually with each player.

"For things to change," Daly later told the *Philadelphia Daily News*, "he had to assume control. And he did."

It was a constant learning process, but Billy picked things up quickly. It also helped that at the end of each season he would gather a stack of videotapes and visit his coaching friends, and they would talk shop. Sometimes it would be Villanova's Rollie Massimino. Sometimes it would be Cal's Lou Campanelli. Often it would be Dean Smith.

After a year and a half, Billy felt he had settled in. Sure, losses continued to stick in his craw. He once wandered the streets of Chicago deep into the night after a defeat. He was eventually stopped by a cop who told him it wasn't safe for him to be in that particular part of town. But Billy's command of the game's technical aspects improved, as did his people skills. No longer did he feel like he was one of the players, even though he was not much older than some of them; professional distance had been established.

"I felt like he improved every year as a coach," Bobby Jones said. "I enjoyed Billy because he didn't play favorites. He played the guys that were getting it done."

"The key thing he had to learn," trainer Al Domenico said, "was the players who are supposed to get their minutes must get their minutes. I think Dean Smith at North Carolina helped Billy understand that. Billy was good at getting players to understand and accept their roles."

Though that wasn't always easy, especially with one player in particular.

"ANDREWWW"

The scenario played out again and again: Billy giving explicit instructions to Andrew Toney, our young, talented guard. Toney ignoring those instructions. Billy stomping down the sideline and screaming "ANDREWWW" at the top of his lungs.

"That was a constant," said a season-ticket holder named Bryan Abrams. "Whether we won 65 games or not, Billy was yelling at Andrew."

"I still remember to this day the other players [on the bench] turning their heads to keep from laughing," retired *Inquirer* columnist Bill Lyon said.

One of the things that made Andrew very good (bordering on great) was also the thing that made him frustrating to coach—his stubbornness. There wasn't a defender he didn't feel he could beat, and there wasn't a shot he didn't believe he could make. Now he was being asked to play in a structured system, to share the ball with players who were his equal. And he was being asked—actually, being told in no uncertain terms—to play defense.

"It's not like he took shortcuts defensively," Guokas said. "Because he was a young player, he didn't have the know-how and the experience. There were a lot of areas where it would look like he was drifting."

So Billy went to great lengths to get him back on track.

"I rode him hard," Cunningham said, "because when you see such greatness, you want to max it out."

And that sometimes brought maximum stress to the head coach.

Earl Cureton, Andrew's closest friend on the team, remembered a night we were getting smoked in Milwaukee. Andrew was having a miserable time of it, missing shot after shot. It didn't stop him from taking them, mind you, but he couldn't get anything going.

So Billy called a timeout and told him to concentrate on running the offense, to let the game come to him.

The timeout ended. The ball was inbounded. And Toney, first chance he got, launched a three-pointer.

Stomp. "ANDREWWW."

"He drove Billy absolutely crazy," Cureton said.

But the thing was, Andrew seemed to follow every mistake with a brilliant play. And over time, he did become a better defender. He did become more well-rounded.

So maybe he really was listening to Billy. Maybe.

TRANSITION GAME

Billy had a roster full of Andrew Toneys his first season. "Good guys," he said, "but everybody wanted to be a star."

"They tested him," Julius Erving said.

It became clear that only a roster shakeup would make the team more defensive-minded, more fast-break-oriented, more Dr. J-centered. And the changes were going to have to start with George McGinnis.

That wasn't going to be easy for any of us, because George had resurrected the Sixers. Signed away from Indiana of the ABA in July 1975 for the princely sum of $2.5 million (over five years), he had given the franchise much-needed credibility in the years after 9-73. He was the marquee talent, the guy who took us back to the playoffs, the guy who gave rise to a new golden age for the team.

"Let George Do It," had been our marketing slogan his first year in town, and for the most part he had. But he was an indifferent practice player, and he had failed spectacularly in the playoffs.

Billy came to the conclusion that George had to go after his first season as coach, a conclusion that left him in a particularly difficult spot. He and George were close. They had played with and against each other, and they were neighbors on the Main Line. George would often stop by the Cunninghams' home, and he and his wife, Lynda, had grown particularly close to one of Billy's daughters.

But it was time. "I felt he'd lost his passion for the game," Billy said, "and once that happens, you can't be good."

We nearly consummated a deal in 1978 that would have sent George back to the Pacers for the first overall pick in the draft—a pick we would have used on North Carolina point guard Phil Ford—but Fitz Dixon pulled the plug when Indiana asked us to pick up some of George's salary. Nor were we able to get anything done with Kansas City, which held the second choice (which the Kings would ultimately use on Ford).

Then Denver Nuggets general manager Carl Scheer called me, offering Bobby Jones.

Scheer had turned down my offer of George for Bobby a year earlier, after Gene Shue had expressed the same sort of dismay about George that Billy ultimately would. But there were concerns about Bobby's health.

He was taking one type of medication for a heart condition, another for epilepsy; in combination they rendered him sluggish. While he had established himself as a premier defender and opportunistic scorer, as a guy who played hard and unselfishly, no one knew if he would be able to maintain that level of play—least of all him.

But after the trade was made, the heart ailment cleared up. Whether that was because he was no longer playing at altitude, no one knew; even his doctors were at a loss. His sluggishness, as a result, disappeared. Bobby was free to be Bobby.

MORE CHANGES

The McGinnis trade cost Billy a friend; he said in a 1988 interview with *PhillySport Magazine* that Big George did not speak to him for the better part of a decade after we sent him to the Nuggets.

But Billy had no regrets.

"It was my job to try and make the 76ers a better basketball team," he said in that same interview. "And the problem was that Julius Erving and George McGinnis did not complement each other. And who was I going to get rid of, McGinnis or Erving? That was an easy decision."

Others proved just as easy, and just as necessary. Like the one to trade World B. Free to the Clippers two months after the McGinnis trade, for a 1984 first-round draft pick (a pick that would ultimately become Charles Barkley). And the one to send Joe Bryant to the Clippers in 1979 for an '86 first-rounder (which would come into play on one of the franchise's darker days).

The draft brought Maurice Cheeks, Clint Richardson, and Andrew Toney in successive years, beginning in 1978. The roster had been reshaped. We were more cohesive. We defended. We ran. And we won, except when it really mattered.

The defeat that gnawed at Billy more than any other was the one to Boston in the 1981 Eastern Conference Finals—up three games to one, one victory away from the Finals, and unable to get it done.

Billy had tried everything to light a fire under his team in the last three games, even going so far as to chew out Julius Erving during a timeout.

"I know when challenged, Julius would go to another level," he said, years later. "I was hoping he would get so mad at me, he'd take it out on the Celtics."

But that didn't work, either. Nothing did.

After the one-point loss in Game 7, Billy sat glumly on the team bus as it crept down an alley outside Boston Garden.

A crowd of Celtics fans blocked the vehicle's way. They began beating on the windows and tearing at the windshield wipers.

"We've got two choices," the driver said to Billy. "Either we go, or we sit here."

Billy told him to plow ahead. It was the only way he knew.

5

The first time Moses Malone donned a Sixers uniform was in a small-college gym in the heart of Amish Country.

It was the first day of training camp, at Franklin & Marshall College in Lancaster, some 90 minutes west of Philadelphia. Moses, wearing his white No. 2 jersey, was surrounded by reporters. The mood was light. (And would remain so. The next day, Moses jogged past Harold Katz during a drill and told him not to worry, because we were going to "win 'bout 70.")

Nobody was bothered when Moses lagged far behind his teammates during the mile run that first day, a run won by Andrew Toney in a blistering five minutes, three seconds.

Nobody seemed bothered by anything. Except this: Maurice Cheeks was nowhere to be found.

He had undergone his pre-camp physical, reported to the team hotel, and then left. His agent, Lance Luchnick, told reporters Maurice was unhappy with his contract, which would pay him $175,000 in 1982-83. That was far less than the salaries of elite point guards like Magic Johnson ($1 million), Gus Williams ($600,000), Norm Nixon ($600,000), and Tiny Archibald ($500,000).

We were unmoved, since Maurice was in the second year of a five-year contract. But we also knew we needed him.

COMPLEMENTARY PLAYERS

Maurice and Andrew, his backcourt partner, were close, which made sense given their skill sets (Maurice was unselfish to a fault, while Andrew never met a shot he didn't like) and similar backgrounds. Both had grown up in inner cities—Maurice in Chicago, Andrew in Birmingham. Both had gone to out-of-the-way schools—West Texas State in the case of Maurice, Southwestern Louisiana in the case of Andrew.

Al Domenico, our trainer, noted one other similarity. "Neither one of them would spend a dime," he said, looking back. "I think they still have their Holy Communion money."

But there were also significant differences. Maurice hadn't always been a star. Andrew had. Maurice was shy. Andrew was bold. Maurice did everything Billy Cunningham asked, as soon as possible. Andrew seemed bent on pushing the envelope, if not tearing it to shreds.

The 1982-83 season was Maurice's fifth in the league, Andrew's third. Whatever questions there had been about Cheeks' leadership ability—questions that had led us to trade for two veteran guards, Eric Money and Al Skinner, his rookie year—were long gone.

"He always made the right play," said retired Milwaukee center Bob Lanier. "He was the quintessential guard. Every time he had it in his hands, he made the right play. He made everyone around him better. I don't think he gets his just due. He was a great, great player who understood his role."

Lionel Hollins, Maurice's teammate early in his career, went so far as to say Cheeks was "[John] Stockton before Stockton." Jack McCallum, *Sports Illustrated's* longtime NBA writer, wouldn't put Cheeks in that class. But he did say Maurice was "the best guy there could have been for that team."

As longtime NBA assistant Dave Wohl once told the *Boston Globe's* Bob Ryan, Cheeks was an "extension of Billy's thoughts on the floor. . . . It's as if Billy hits Maurice's neurons, and they correlate. It's like computer language."

Maurice played tidy, mistake-free ball, pushing the pace when it needed to be pushed, slowing it down when it needed to be slowed. He knew when and where his teammates should get the ball, and knew when to look for his own shot.

"If he made a mistake, you almost fell off your chair," recalled Don Benevento of the *Camden Courier-Post*. "He was probably the foundation of that team. You've got Malone, Erving, and Toney, and he always seemed to know who to get it to."

Just as he always knew what he had to do at the other end of the court: "There was no more dangerous defender in the league," said Ryan, who proclaimed himself "regional president of the Maurice Cheeks Fan Club."

Lester Conner broke in with Golden State in '82-83 and played point guard for seven teams over the course of his 12 seasons. He recalled that Cheeks would "pick me up fullcourt and funnel me any direction he wanted."

"I didn't like playing against him, I really didn't," remembered Doc Rivers, who began his 13-year career with Atlanta in '83-84. "He was one of the guys who made it very difficult to throw the ball to the post. . . . Maurice and [former San Antonio guard] Alvin Robertson were really the only two guys that I didn't enjoy bringing the ball up the court on, because Maurice had that Walt Frazier ability to pick guys at halfcourt. He made me uncomfortable."

Cheeks admittedly played possum with guys, letting them easily advance the ball early in games, then turning up the heat as the night wore on. He doesn't remember whether he did that to Rivers the first time he faced him, but he made an immediate impression nonetheless.

"He got me late," Rivers said two decades after the fact.

Dribbling upcourt in the closing minute of a tight game in the Omni, then the Hawks' home arena, Rivers looked over at coach Mike Fratello for the play call. And just like that, Rivers said, "The ball was gone."

Happened all the time.

"[Cheeks] was one of the key guys in taking games over," Matty Guokas said. "He usually did it defensively, with a steal or deflection. That would generate defensive intensity, and off we'd go."

UNLIKELY TREK

No way should Maurice have been in a position to harass Doc Rivers or Lester Conner or anyone of that caliber. No way should he have been anywhere near an NBA arena without a ticket in hand.

But that's where William Dise comes in. He was the star center at Chicago's DuSable High in the mid-'70s, a guy who was being recruited by West Texas State coach Ron Ekker.

Dise finally told Ekker he would come to school, but he had one question: Could he bring his point guard along with him?

Ekker said he could.

Dise's reasoning was simple: "If you have someone who butters your bread, you keep him around," he said years later, having settled in Denver, where he worked as an operations supervisor for American Airlines.

Cheeks had not started at DuSable until his senior year, and only Division II Eastern Illinois had expressed even the slightest interest in him. But DuSable coach Bob Bonner told Ekker that when all was said and done, he would like Cheeks more than Dise.

That proved prophetic. Dise left school after a year, and later resurfaced at DePaul. Cheeks wanted to leave, too; the move from the projects of Chicago—the infamous Robert Taylor homes, once described as "the place where hope goes to die"—to Canyon, Texas (population 9,000) was more than he could take.

But his mom wouldn't let him leave, and he developed into a three-time All-Missouri Valley Conference Player, not to mention a beloved figure in the area. He worked with kids on the playgrounds of nearby Amarillo in the summertime, and he played pickup ball with the high school guys, too.

And one day before his senior year (1977-78) he was passing through a West Texas gym when he saw a young girl shooting around.

"You call that a layup?" he asked, good-naturedly.

He offered to work with the girl, whose name was Michele Telfair. Her mom, Laurie, a local newspaper reporter, asked around, just to make sure his intentions were honorable. Everyone assured her: Maurice is the best.

He didn't transform Michele, then a seventh-grader, into a star or anything; she gave up organized ball a year or two later. But he did become a friend of the family. And Laurie and Michele frequented his games.

They were driving home after a game them late in Cheeks' final season when they heard Ekker being interviewed on the radio. West Texas was en route to an 8-19 finish, and the coach was saying that it was a shame Cheeks had gone unnoticed by NBA scouts.

But that could be rectified, Ekker added, if the fans voted their point guard into something called the Pizza Hut Classic. Other teams' rooters were doing it, goodness knows, but not those in Canyon.

"That's the first time I knew there was a Pizza Hut game," Laurie Telfair said. (And indeed, there isn't one anymore.)

Through some connections she got her hands on some ballots, and before long people were filling them out everywhere: at games, in dorms, in junior high study halls. A town of 9,000 created a 400,000-vote landslide for their candidate.

"Everybody liked him," Laurie recalled. "He was a sweet-natured person. Everyone was happy to do it."

Cheeks played rings around Marquette All-American Butch Lee in the game, which was great news for the folks in Canyon, but did not appear to be the best news for us.

Jack McMahon, our cheif scout, had scouted Maurice early in his senior season and liked him. Jack always favored guards who could get to the rim, his reasoning being that only good things happened off penetration. And Maurice, while not the accomplished jump-shooter he would later become, could always break his man down off the dribble. Jack was also sure Cheeks could make the transition from West Texas State's methodical offense to our racehorse style.

So for a very long time Maurice was our little secret, a guy we were sure we could steal on draft day—though we were hoping to get a crack at North Carolina All-American Phil Ford.

Our attempts to trade George McGinnis for one of the first two picks failed, however. And once Cheeks played so well in the Pizza Hut game, we feared we wouldn't get a crack at him, either. But he was still there in the second round, at No. 36 overall, and we happily gobbled him up. He would remain a Sixer for the next 11 years and play 15 seasons in all.

Ford? He was named Rookie of the Year in 1978-79, and enjoyed two more productive years with the Kings. But he bounced around to three other teams and was out of the league by 1985.

Lee? He was taken 10th overall that year, by Atlanta, and had an undistinguished four-year career.

MO BETTER

Long after his playing career ended, Cheeks would describe himself as someone who had "always been more in the back seat."

"Always have been," he said. "It's always worked for me."

That doesn't mean he was just along for the ride, though. It just means he went out of his way to make the trip more enjoyable for everyone else, that he would seek to make the unselfish play, the winning play.

Very early in his career he gravitated toward Caldwell Jones, whose own ideas of how the game should be played meshed with Cheeks'. As Caldwell said, "I enjoy winning. If I could score less and win, I was happy. Playing basketball's a lot more fun when you're winning."

Everything Cheeks did was geared toward improving himself, and by extension, the team. When Billy Cunningham told him he needed to become more of a leader, he went back to Chicago and played on the youngest summer-league team. And because he knew opponents would challenge him to make outside shots (especially in the trench warfare of the playoffs), he worked tirelessly on his jumper. Because of that, and because he was such a terrific finisher on the break, he shot 52.3 percent from the field in the course of his career.

He knew how to pick his spots, too: "He could score eight points," Doc Rivers said, "but all eight of those points were [courtesy of] big shots. Big shots to me are when [an opponent] makes an 8-0 run on you in the first quarter and you come down and pop an elbow jumpshot, which he would do on the fast break. Then he wouldn't shoot for a while, but he stopped the run. To me Maurice understood his role as well as anybody."

He was never comfortable talking about it, though. When reporters approached him after a game, he would bow his head, study the locker-room floor, and answer their questions in a whisper—and sometimes not even that.

One time Sam Smith, who worked for Maurice's hometown paper, the *Chicago Tribune*, wanted to do an interview. Cheeks begged off.

"Those are the guys you want to talk to," Cheeks said, gesturing in the direction of his teammates.

Smith insisted he did not, that what he really wanted to do was write about Maurice. It did no good.

"I couldn't get him to talk," Smith recalled. "He was so humble about himself."

QUICK RESOLUTION

Harold Katz and I reopened the lines of communication with Maurice shortly after camp began in an impromptu meeting at the Bellevue-Stratford Hotel in downtown Philadelphia. We huddled for 30 minutes amid the clutter of a recently used ballroom; Harold was still wearing his tux from the charity dinner he had just attended.

Maurice Cheeks handles the ball against Norm Nixon during Game 3 of the Finals.
Philadelphia Daily News/George Reynolds

We told Maurice there would be no renegotiation, and no extension.

He was in camp the next day, telling reporters that there had been a miscommunication. Harold, meanwhile, declared that he would never deal with Lance Luchnick again.

"He's an arrogant person," Katz told reporters, "and I don't need that."

6

Andrew Toney first saw Boston Garden when the Sixers played there his rookie year (1980-81). And this is what he said as he disembarked from the team bus and looked upon one of the most storied arenas ever built, the gritty cathedral where Russell and Cousy and Bird had held sway for so many years: "Where the gym at?"

It was, to the young shooting guard, just another gym. Just another proving ground. No need to be in awe.

Toney—soon to be dubbed "The Boston Strangler," a nickname he inherited from World B. Free—treated the Celtics with similar disdain, scoring 35 points in a game against them his first year, 25 points against them in a single quarter his second season, and 39 points in Game 4 of the '81-82 Eastern Conference Finals.

Game 7 of that series was a winner-take-all scrum in the Garden after we'd blown a three-games-to-one lead. Andrew was never better, shrugging off the grinding pressure (and whatever memory he might have had of his 1-for-11 shooting performance in Game 6 two days earlier) to score 34 points in a 120-106 victory, which launched us into the Finals.

The key moment came midway through the third quarter. After starting quickly behind Andrew's 14 first-quarter points and leading most of the way, we now faced another in a series of Boston challenges: eight straight Celtics points to cut our lead from ten to two, at 64-62.

The Garden was rocking. Billy Cunningham was raging, at one point storming over to the scorers' table to tell the stat guys that a foul was on reserve forward Mike Bantom, not Toney. (Television replays seemed to indicate otherwise.)

Moments later, the CBS-TV cameras flashed to a green-and-white banner hanging from the arena's upper deck. "Déjà Vu," it said, a reference to the year before, when the Celtics had come from 3-1 down to beat the Sixers in seven games, en route to the championship.

Enter Andrew.

As Maurice Cheeks handled the ball at the head of the key, Toney maneuvered on the left wing. Celtics defender M.L. Carr jostled him—too much, in the opinion of assistant coach Jack McMahon, who sprang from the bench to bark at the referees.

Toney finally collected the ball at the top of the circle and started right, slowly at first, then accelerating after he lost Carr on Caldwell Jones' screen. Then, unbothered by an onrushing Robert Parish, he swished a 12-footer from the side of the lane.

Two more Sixers baskets followed, then a Carr stick-back.

"Secondary," Billy yelled, meaning the secondary fast break.

This time Toney, moving from right to left along the baseline, ran Carr around picks by Bantom, Jones, and Julius Erving before taking Cheeks' pass in the left corner, squaring up and connecting.

Parish answered with two free throws. And then, once more: "Secondary."

This time Erving set the only screen, but the effect was the same: Andrew hit a jumper, deeper in the left corner this time.

Now the lead was eight. It was 12 after three quarters, and the Celtics began the final period by putting a big lineup on the court. Meaning that none other than Larry Bird was playing Andrew.

Early on, there was a three-point play, when Toney lost Bird on Bobby Jones screen and nailed yet another jumper, this one while being fouled by Cedric Maxwell. Moments later, Andrew dribbled down the left side of the court, ignored a wide-open Julius Erving as he waved for the ball on the opposite wing, and scored again. So much for Larry Bird.

Now it was back to rookie Danny Ainge, who had played Andrew earlier, but who admitted years later that Toney "struck fear into [him] like no one else."

Once more: "Secondary."

This time Ainge fought his way through traffic and was right up on Toney as he handled the ball on the left baseline, 12 feet from the basket.

One pump fake. Then another. Then a pivot, and another pump fake.

And another swish.

A subsequent Toney basket brought the lead to 17 with a little over five minutes remaining.

Now the Sixers were up and celebrating. Now it was just a matter of time.

REVOLVING DOOR

Besides Carr, Ainge, and, on occasion, Bird, the Celtics used Chris Ford against Andrew early in his career. Also Gerald Henderson. Everyone, it seemed, but Red Auerbach. Before the 1982-83 campaign Boston traded fading star Dave Cowens to Milwaukee for Quinn Buckner, a fine defensive guard. Buckner would have as much luck as his predecessors.

Toney was "a killer" in the estimation of ex-Celtics coach K.C. Jones. Maybe even the Devil; that's how some within the Boston organization referred to Toney, according to another former coach, Bill Fitch.

Fitch recalled that Toney was one of the first players he felt compelled to double-team. Not that it mattered.

"He could flat out light it up, and we weren't able to handle him," said yet another retired Boston coach, Jimmy Rodgers.

"I've always said that Magic [Johnson], Michael [Jordan] and Isiah [Thomas] were the greatest players I went up against," Ainge said, "but Andrew was not far off."

There are those who believe Andrew—not Julius Erving, not Moses Malone—was the best offensive player on the '82-83 Sixers. And you could make an awfully strong case. Just 25 that season, he was two years younger than Moses, seven years younger than Doc. He had a blinding first step and limitless range on his unusual-looking jumper, which he released in front of his face.

Andrew was strong. He could run all day. And, said Franklin Edwards, a backup guard on the title team, "He was mean. On the court he had a nasty attitude. He felt if you couldn't guard him, you shouldn't be on him."

Which narrowed the field considerably.

"I don't think there was such a thing as overconfidence when it came to him," Edwards said. "He believed he could make every shot. He's the only guy I ever played with who believed he could make every shot."

WHO'S GOT NEXT?

Toney and Edwards would drive around in the summer, looking for pickup games all over Philadelphia. Edwards said there would be times when the other players might be surprised to see them, but there would never be a problem. "And," Frank said, "we went into some rough neighborhoods."

Mostly the locals would want to shake hands, get an autograph, talk a little ball. And play. Especially that.

"We would get [to a place] at two and stay until seven," Edwards said. "They were great games. Players in Philadelphia don't care who you are."

And sometimes they didn't know. One day, Edwards and Toney were shooting around in Saint Joseph University's fieldhouse, where the Sixers practiced during the season. Two younger, taller kids, maybe 6-foot-7 or so, were shooting around at the basket at the far end of the court, so Frank and Andrew walked down and asked if they wanted to play two-on-two.

As Edwards remembers it, the two kids started laughing.

"Why don't we break it up?" one of them said.

Toney informed them the teams were fine the way they were. So they played three games, each of them one-sided victories for Frank and Andrew.

"By the time we finished the third game, they were like, 'What in the heck happened?'" Edwards said. "They never asked us who we were. They just walked out of the gym. They looked so puzzled, like, 'These two little guys just beat us.'"

EQUAL-OPPORTUNITY ASSASSIN

The way Philadelphia sportscaster Howard Eskin sees it, Toney's designation as the Boston Strangler was woefully inadequate.

"Really," Eskin said, "he strangled everyone. He had a weird-looking shot, but he had the most guts of any player I ever saw. He was never afraid to take a big shot, and most of the time he hit them."

"Andrew Toney gave me nightmares," recalled Sidney Moncrief, then an All-Star guard for Milwaukee. "He was one of the most complete NBA guards ever. He had that quick first step that allowed him to go quickly to the hoop. Or he'd plant himself and get off that mid-range jumper that

Andrew Toney honestly thought he could make every shot. Here he tries one against Magic Johnson and Kareem Abdul-Jabbar. *Philadelphia Daily News/George Reynolds*

you couldn't defend. Offensively, there was nothing Andrew couldn't do, and he didn't need a lot of shots to do his damage."

Toney's career high of 46 points came in his second year, against the Lakers and Michael Cooper, one of the finest perimeter defenders of his day. Cooper, looking back two decades later, said that if Larry Bird was the toughest guy he ever guarded, Andrew was second.

"He was one of the most fearless scorers," Cooper said. "You couldn't intimidate him, any kind of way. . . . If that team had not been loaded with the stars they had, he could have easily led the league in scoring."

Toney came off the bench his first two years while Lionel Hollins started alongside Maurice Cheeks. But Hollins broke his left hand in a fight with Tree Rollins during a first-round playoff series against Atlanta in '81-82, and Andrew became the starter.

That wasn't going to change the following year, so we traded Hollins— the highest-paid guard on our team at $365,000 a year—to the Clippers.

Edwards, entering his second year, would now get regular minutes as Cheeks' backup. Clint Richardson, an athletic, defensive-minded fourth-year man, would remain the primary reserve behind Andrew.

BURGEONING REPUTATION

Though he played at Southwestern Louisiana, Andrew was hardly a secret. Everybody had been down to scout him. Jack McMahon saw Toney in a holiday tournament his senior year—or, at least, saw the first night of the tournament. Having witnessed a typical Andrew explosion, he didn't bother to go back the second night. He had seen enough.

George Shirk, working for the *Des Moines Register* (prior to his stint on the Sixers beat for the *Philadelphia Inquirer*), also saw Andrew that year, in an NCAA Tournament game against a Kevin McHale-led Minnesota team. The Gophers won, but Toney's performance, George decided, was "like a rocket attack."

A few months later, Matty Guokas' wife, Barb, accompanied her husband to a postseason tournament in Hawaii after Jack McMahon fell ill. Matty asked which players stood out in her mind.

"No. 32 and No. 22 look pretty good to me," she said. No. 32 was McHale, who had a great career with Boston. No. 22 was Andrew.

"They were playing at a different level than everyone else," Matty recalled. "We had the eighth pick in that draft, and I thought after Hawaii we'd never see Andrew there."

Especially since the Nets also liked Toney, and they owned the two picks immediately before ours. But draft night brought a surprise. New Jersey took North Carolina forward Mike O'Koren at No. 6, and Duke center Mike Gminski at No. 7.

Andrew Toney had fallen into our laps.

"I want you to know we're giving you an NBA title," Nets general manager Charlie Theokas told me over the phone. "When you win it, order a ring for me."

IMMEDIATE IMPACT

Andrew swept through his first training camp like a tornado, uprooting veterans and changing the landscape of the team.

Henry Bibby, who had played in our backcourt the previous four years (and had logged eight NBA seasons in all), immediately realized the enormity of the challenge the newcomer presented.

"I remember him being so strong," Henry said. "Strong and mentally tough—that's what he was. He knew he could beat you. And he would beat you, and then he would let you know he beat you."

As a result, Bibby said, "He took a lot of my confidence, because he was so good."

Also because Toney was good and ticked off. Earl Cureton, who was also in his first season, recalled that Andrew was Bibby's rookie, meaning that he had to run all sorts of errands for the veteran. Toney quickly tired of such demands, and he exacted his revenge in practice.

Really, though, he spared no one. One day Bibby asked Hollins why he didn't guard Toney the way he guarded him, and Hollins told him that Andrew was "a different breed of bird."

"It wasn't like I wasn't trying to guard Andrew Toney; I couldn't guard Andrew Toney," Hollins recalled. "Andrew was an offensive talent I had never seen before."

The opponents Lionel had always been asked to defend—guys like George Gervin, David Thompson and Brian Winters—all had weaknesses he could exploit. But he had a devil of a time finding any in Andrew. That lower-than-normal release on his jumper? A non-issue. He was so quick and strong, he had no problem creating the necessary space to launch.

Henry was cut at the end of camp. The newcomer was everything we had envisioned.

Jack McMahon, who had coached Oscar Robertson with the Cincinnati Royals, once told Phil Jasner that while he did not wish to compare anyone to the Big O, Andrew was similar in a couple of specific ways, most notably his "innate ability to get from Point A to Point B" whenever he wanted.

And it didn't seem to matter who was in his way. Toney once told Edwards that he didn't think so much about the defender assigned to him, because he knew he could beat him; he was more concerned with the other guys, the guys who might offer help.

"That's confidence," Frank said.

Toney displayed that in other ways, too. Early in his rookie year, his teammates were shocked when he waved Julius Erving out of the low post, so that he would have more room to go one-on-one with his defender.

"Nobody would do that to Doc," Hollins said, "let alone a rookie."

Cureton reminded Toney of what he had done, and to whom he had done it.

"He's leaving, though," he said, unmoved.

7

Bobby Jones did not regard the 1982-83 season as anything special. That's because he regarded every season that way. It stands to reason, given his affliction, and given his faith.

"When I got epilepsy, I didn't know how long I was going to [play]," he said in April 2006. "Every year was an opportunity to do something the Lord blessed me with. It was something I didn't take for granted, or tried not to."

Trainer Al Domenico described Jones as "the only born-again guy I know who's born again," Yet Bobby played like a demon. He would go hurtling into scorer's tables, fly downcourt on the break, mix it up inside with players 30 pounds heavier. He was, as Lakers coach Pat Riley said, "the quintessential NBA player of all time."

While well intentioned, that statement wasn't entirely true. Bobby hated the arrogance and selfishness that ran rampant in the league. But he loved to compete, loved to win.

Clark Kellogg, a rookie forward for the Indiana Pacers in 1982-83, understood that right away. While Bobby—gaunt, chalky, hollow-cheeked—didn't look like much, Kellogg said he was "hardnosed . . . soft-spoken, but really hardnosed."

"Anybody who plays at the level he played at, despite the soft-spoken demeanor, is a hard guy," Kellogg added. "There's a hardness to him. There's a toughness. There's a focus. There's a tenacity to him. It just doesn't manifest itself in the ways it does in other people. But you can't deny it."

Kellogg noted that every night, Bobby had to joust with big-time scorers like Bernard King, Adrian Dantley, and Alex English. And more often than not, he was equal to the task.

"Eighty percent of [defending] is wanting to try to stop your guy," Kellogg said. "The other part of it is what you have athletically. And he had good feet, good length and range, and terrific anticipation."

Kellogg, who weighed 230 pounds, knew that if he could get his body on Bobby, who spread 210 pounds over his 6-foot-9 frame, he could overpower him near the basket. But that was easier said than done.

"He was so good at breaking contact and anticipating, and trying to beat you to spots," Kellogg said. "And he had good players around him. But basically, individually, I think it was his range, his anticipation, his want-to, and his quickness [that set him apart]."

Some called Bobby "The White Shadow." Julius Erving considered him his "vice president." The irrepressible Darryl Dawkins had his own nickname for Bobby: "White Lightning." That's because he was, in Darryl's estimation, the "baddest white dude in the whole league."

DEVELOPING SITUATION

Growing up in Charlotte, North Carolina, Bobby had scant interest in basketball. He played only because his father, who had played at Oklahoma, and his older brother, who would later do the same, goaded him into joining them on the tiny backyard court.

"It was an awkward time for me," Bobby remembered. "I wasn't very coordinated. As a middle schooler I would see NBA games on TV and think that was the farthest thing I could ever do in my life. Seven or eight years later, I was in the league."

He was in sixth grade when he began to come around. His dad would intentionally fire passes at Bobby's feet, and he would snag them, leading both to understand that he had sure hands, that he wasn't nearly as awkward as either one of them believed.

And because the right side of the Jones' court had been washed away by rain, Bobby began to develop his left-handed shot, something which later became one of his trademarks.

A reporter named Mark Whicker, who would one day document much of Bobby's pro career as a columnist for the *Philadelphia Daily News*, first covered him at South Mecklenburg High School while working for a paper in Chapel Hill, North Carolina. Whicker said Bobby was the same then as he would be later: unselfish, tough, and tenacious.

He landed at the University of North Carolina, where he fit in beautifully with Dean Smith's share-the-wealth system. The ball would come to him, and Bobby would whip it to another teammate almost immediately. That was partly because that was what Smith asked of his players, and partly because Bobby, by his own admission, had "never learned how to dribble very well."

But Bobby was always an accurate shooter, never forcing things, always working within the structure of the offense. And always thankful.

He became known for a simple gesture—the finger point—every time a teammate set him up for a basket. He was, in fact, "the best pointer in NBA history," as broadcaster Steve Jones informed his television audience during a game early in the 2005-06 season. Steve knew that as well as anyone, having played against Bobby in the ABA.

"He would point even if he missed," Steve told viewers, "He would thank, and thank again."

"It's a team game," Bobby said. "You don't score by yourself. Even if I missed a layup, I would thank someone for the pass. It wasn't his fault I missed. It was just a show of appreciation."

BREAKING-IN PERIOD

When Bobby first came to Philadelphia, the fans didn't fully understand or appreciate what he was all about. They had grown accustomed to George McGinnis' scoring binges. His replacement, they found, did things very differently. But grit had always played well in the Delaware Valley, and that would again prove to be the case.

"Bobby was about as Philadelphia a player as there was," said season-ticket holder Bryan Abrams.

"He didn't know how to lose," said former *Inquirer* beat writer George Shirk. "[Losing] was so against the grain of what he was. He would have his left leg right at every opponent's jaw when he went in for a layup. He was a fearsome player in that he knew how to position his body. He was 6-9, and it was all knee coming at you. You got in the way of that at your own peril. He would lead with his elbow and his knee."

BENCHMARK

Bobby was a starter his first season with us, but before the second, Billy Cunningham thought about asking him to come off the bench. Billy figured it would not be an easy sell, but he thought that if he sat down with Bobby and patiently explained he wanted to go with a bigger lineup, featuring Darryl Dawkins and Caldwell Jones, Bobby would grudgingly accept a new role.

Training camp came. Cunningham approached Bobby, armed with all his arguments. He didn't need them. "It took him about 30 seconds to agree," Billy remembered. "If I had known that, I wouldn't have worried about it all summer."

By the championship season—a season that would see him named the inaugural Sixth Man of the Year—Bobby was one of the most feared subs in the league.

"The guy would be sitting on the side in a game or practice and be completely out of it," said John Kilbourne, our strength and conditioning coach that year. "Billy would yell, 'Bobby,' and it was just like night and day. Bobby would jump up and be on fire."

"When I think of Bobby, I think of how brave he is," said Mark McNamara, a backup center in '82-83. "He felt a low-grade malaise, and he just rose above it. He went out and played like a brave warrior. . . . He was one of the key factors. He was one of those guys who made you say, 'Without him, I don't know [if we win it].'"

TRUSTY SIDEKICK

Next off the bench after Bobby was his friend Clint Richardson, a player whose career I nearly nipped in the bud.

The players liked to say that I carried a Bible in one hand, a hatchet in the other—the first because of my beliefs, the second because I often had the unenviable task of paring the roster. And the hatchet I carried to a 1979 preseason game in Pittsburgh came in the form of a plane ticket.

A one-way ticket to Seattle—Clint's hometown—with his name on it.

He had been our second-round draft pick that year, but his transition from college small forward to NBA guard had not gone well. Moreover, we had depth and experience in the backcourt: Maurice Cheeks and Doug Collins as starters, Henry Bibby and Eric Money behind them. So it fell

Their night's work done, Bobby Jones (left) and Clint Richardson relax on the bench late in a playoff game against Milwaukee. *Philadelphia Daily News/George Reynolds*

upon me to give him the bad news that we would no longer require his services.

Clint played well that night, though, and wound up making the team. He would later start 34 games when Collins was hurt, only to return to the bench when we traded for Lionel Hollins, and over the next two years his role would constantly change. Sometimes he played a lot. Sometimes he didn't play at all.

He finally became the third guard in the 1981-82 playoffs, when Hollins broke his hand in a fight with Tree Rollins, and remained in that role the following year when we traded Hollins to the Clippers.

At 6-foot-4, Clint was long-armed and athletic, a perfect guy to defend bigger guards, like George Gervin, Sidney Moncrief, and Magic Johnson. And a perfect sidekick to Bobby.

"We had similar personalities," Bobby said. "He was down-to-earth and easygoing. He enjoyed coming off the bench. . . . It worked out well."

8

Marc Iavaroni was a rookie forward with the 1982-83 Sixers, a 26-year-old trying to find a niche in the league after several false starts. But as he took the floor in Knoxville, Tennessee, for a preseason game against Boston, it quickly became apparent that this was not just another chance to impress the coaches. This was survival: Sixers-Celtics, the preeminent rivalry in sports.

"They went right at me," he recalled.

Again and again veteran forward Cedric Maxwell posted up Iavaroni in front of the Boston bench. And again and again Iavaroni heard the taunts from those seated there: "UH-OH! UH-OH! TORTURE CHAMBER! TORTURE CHAMBER!" Before the game was six minutes old, Maxwell had ten points, and Iavaroni had four fouls.

It would get no better for Iavaroni the rest of the night. Later, after the game, he walked past the coffee shop of the hotel the Sixers and Celtics shared. The coffee shop was now occupied by several Celtics.

"UH-OH! UH-OH! TORTURE CHAMBER! TORTURE CHAMBER!"

Welcome to the NBA, rook.

YOUNGER—AND CHEAPER

We kept four rookies at the beginning of the '82-83 season—a team record—the idea being that we needed younger, less expensive players to offset Moses Malone's cumbersome salary. Veteran forwards Steve Mix and

Mike Bantom were not re-signed. Guard Lionel Hollins was traded to the Clippers two days before the season opener.

Replacing them were our first-round pick, Mark McNamara, a free-spirited reserve center from Cal-Berkeley, second-round picks Mitchell Anderson and Russ Schoene, and Iavaroni. All of them found out right away what they had gotten themselves into, the reminders provided not only by rivals like Boston, but also by the Sixers themselves.

Early in training camp, at Franklin & Marshall College in Lancaster, Pennsylvania, some of the newcomers stopped to watch Julius Erving execute a drill. Jack McMahon, the avuncular assistant coach, sidled over to them.

"I know," he said gently. "I could stand and watch him all day, too. But you guys need to be playing."

"That struck me," Schoene said looking back.

Erving himself delivered the same message at just about the same time. He told the rookies it helped no one if they remained star-struck.

"For us to be good, you've got to get over that," he told them. "You've got to come right after us."

"There was a high degree of commitment," McNamara said. "It was very serious from the start, right from the get-go. Everybody had bought in. The superstars led the way. They practiced harder than anybody else.

"There was no slacking. It was 100 percent commitment by a group of guys, the coaching staff, the ownership and really, the whole city."

RAMBIS 2.0

The coaching staff envisioned Iavaroni filling the same role journeyman forward Kurt Rambis had filled with the Lakers—that of banger, pick-setter, and rebounder. Iavaroni, like Rambis, would be expected to start and play the first quarter, then a few minutes at the beginning of the third. The rest of the time Bobby Jones would be on the floor. It was a way to soak up minutes and fouls in a less critical part of the game and save Bobby for the most important times.

Billy Cunningham, Iavaroni remembered, "was determined to have a set rotation. He was committed to it."

Veteran Earl Cureton and rookie free agent Charles Jones (Caldwell's

Marc Iavaroni stands his ground against Washington forward Charles Davis.
Philadelphia Daily News/George Reynolds

younger brother) were also possibilities for the Rambis role. But Cureton was still recovering from a broken foot, an injury he had suffered while jogging over the summer. And Charles, who would eventually enjoy a long career, was still raw. So very early in camp, Marc began working with the starters.

"I was happy to be there," he said, "but I certainly didn't want to make it look like a charity thing."

"THE NEXT SHOT"

Originally a third-round pick of the Knicks in 1978, Marc had failed to stick there, that season or the next. He also flunked tryouts in Portland and Washington, and spent parts of three seasons playing in Italy.

Marc remembers he would hold his own against NBA players in summer-league play, then freeze up when he faced them in a camp setting. His confidence would evaporate. He played neither as aggressively nor as alertly as he did in the unstructured, free-flowing setting.

But he felt different playing for us. It had felt different from the moment Billy Cunningham approached him after a summer-league game in Los Angeles—a game in which Iavaroni's dunk on Orlando Woolridge "got some people's attention," he said—and asked him to come to our rookie camp.

Marc had planned to go to Detroit's camp, but ours preceded that one, so he took Billy up on the offer. Asked years later if he viewed it as his last shot, Iavaroni said, "I looked at it as the next shot. I didn't have some kind of biological clock going."

Things went well in mini-camp, and he received an invitation to veterans' camp. "I felt like I belonged," he said. "I had to make sure I played like that."

He did have some anxiety over what to call Julius Erving. Was "Julius" OK? "Doc"? "Mr. Erving"?

"Doc" was just fine. "[Erving] made you feel like you belonged—that you were his buddy, his peer," Iavaroni said. "He never made you feel like he was superior."

There was a drill early on, and Iavaroni turned to Erving, who was behind him in line. "Make sure I know what to do," he said to Doc.

"You already know what to do," Erving told him.

CHAPTER 8

FRANK TALK

Franklin Edwards wasn't a rookie, but he might as well have been. He had played all of 291 minutes over 42 games in 1981-82, his first season in the league, as the deepest of subs behind Maurice Cheeks, Andrew Toney, Lionel Hollins, and Clint Richardson. But when we traded Hollins on the eve of the '82-83 season, Harold Katz sidled over to Frank after practice.

"I don't want you to feel any pressure," Katz told him, "but don't make a liar out of me."

Frank believed he was ready. He had been practicing against the veterans—Cheeks in particular—for a year. "By then," Frank said, "he wasn't destroying me every day. I was holding my own."

Edwards appreciated the fact that Cheeks and Toney "never let [him] feel [he] wasn't part of what [the team was] doing." And he took it to heart when Billy and Julius told him to stay ready for the moment when his opportunity arrived. Now it was here.

No pressure, though.

PERFECT OMEN

We had done our homework on Frank, who'd scored over 2,000 points at Cleveland State and became the first player in school history to have his number retired. Jack McMahon and Chuck Daly had gone to see him. I had, too.

Frank was quick. He could handle and shoot. And he was unselfish; the only time his coach, Ray Dieringer, grew frustrated with him was when he passed up shots, as he did in his next-to-last college game, at Xavier. Frank had scored 49 points, one shy of the fieldhouse record, but when faced with a two-on-one fast break late in the game, he passed the ball to a seldom-used reserve, instead of taking the shot himself.

While visiting Frank one last time in May 1981, I decided to take in the Indians-Blue Jays game. Tickets weren't hard to come by; I was one of just 7,290 fans rattling around inside cavernous Municipal Stadium that night. But we all witnessed a little slice of history. Cleveland's Len Barker became just the 10th pitcher to work a perfect game that night, beating Toronto 3-0 in a little over two hours.

EAT AND REACT

We used the 22nd pick of the 1981 draft on Frank. Knowing how stacked we were in the backcourt, he was less than thrilled.

"I thought to myself, 'There goes my pro career,'" he said.

He was even less thrilled when he sat in on our contract negotiations with his agent, Ron Grinker, in July.

"My advice to a player is, never do that," Frank said. "You say to yourself, 'Why did they take me?' All you hear from [the team] is what you can't do."

We hammered things out, reluctantly agreeing to include a clause that would guarantee the contract in case of death. Then Frank and I went to dinner at a restaurant partially owned by Billy Cunningham. Edwards rose to go to the men's room and told me to order for him the same thing I was having—flounder stuffed with crabmeat.

From there I whisked him over to Temple's McGonigle Hall, where he would play in a Baker League game. But before long he complained of shortness of breath. He was removed from the game; presumably he wasn't in the best of shape. But his condition did not improve after several minutes on the bench. Now there was real concern. The paramedics were called. The small crowd stirred, and Edwards was taken off the court to an anteroom for treatment. Reporters gathered. They had come to see the Sixers' No. 1 pick perform; now it appeared he was gravely ill.

Spectators guessed that Edwards must have been done in by some food he bought from a street vendor. In reality, crabmeat was the culprit; Frank had had an allergic reaction to it. Once the doctors figured that out, all of us could exhale again.

A FRIENDLY FACE

That first year, Frank gravitated to Caldwell Jones, a man who treated him "like a son."

"I was the only rookie on the team," Edwards said. "That can be a lonely place. No one wants to deal with a rookie."

Caldwell did. So did another veteran, Ollie Johnson. When the team was on the road, Frank would hang with those guys—go to dinner, take in a movie, whatever. But as the '82-83 season began, Caldwell was gone, and gone to a hapless Houston club.

"That's not only irony," Frank said, "but bad irony."

9

Jack McMahon, who in his role as super scout had done so much to assemble the team, did just as much to keep everything from going to pieces. Especially where the head coach was concerned.

"He had the ability to put his arm around me and say, 'OK, kid, nice and easy,'" Billy Cunningham remembered. "He just put everything in the proper perspective, almost like a father."

Everyone gravitated toward Jack—players, fellow coaches, even writers.

"He was the grandfather of the team," said John Kilbourne, the strength and conditioning coach in '82-83. "He was a calming influence. He was the bridge between the players and Billy. He was the wise elder."

Jack visited remote outposts like Canyon, Texas, to scout Maurice Cheeks, and Lafayette, Louisiana, to get a look at Andrew Toney. He went because seeing them in person was the best way to gauge a player; video could only tell you so much. To see a player in the flesh was to see how he interacted with his teammates, how he responded to coaching, how he dealt with adversity.

So he always went, and that made him, in the estimation of one-time *Inquirer* beat writer George Shirk, "a good talent evaluator and a good human evaluator."

Jack once told the *Daily News* that the only time he minded the travel was "when the guy you're scouting turns out to be a stiff."

He missed on occasion, as when we used No. 1 picks on Glenn Mosley and Jim Spanarkel—and years later, Leo Rautins, a player he liked so much he would have taken him ahead of Clyde Drexler, if it had come to that.

But Jack was right far more often than he was wrong. He encouraged the selection of Darryl Dawkins, a high school player out of Orlando, in 1975. He recommended that we take Lloyd [later World B.] Free the same year after he saw Free go to the line 27 times while playing for tiny Guilford College in an AAU Tournament game.

One time Jack was scouting two players from Nevada-Reno, Johnny High and Edgar Jones, both of whom later played in the NBA. But the guy who caught his eye that night was an undersized sophomore forward for Reno's opponent, Seattle.

Which is how we first caught wind of Clint Richardson.

"He flew back with us," Clint recalled. "An assistant coach came back and said, 'A guy from the Philadelphia 76ers is on the plane. They want to find out more about you.'"

Clint, who wound up breaking Elgin Baylor's career scoring record at Seattle, was our second-round choice in 1979.

LONG-TIMER

Jack had been around the league forever it seemed, first as a pass-first, shoot-seldom guard for the old Rochester Royals and St. Louis Hawks, then as a head coach for four teams—most notably the Cincinnati Royals, where he worked with the great Oscar Robertson—and finally as a scout.

The Sixers hired him late in the 1972-73 season (the year they went 9-73), meaning he would have a hand in deciding which player the team would draft No. 1 overall. He liked Doug Collins, a skinny guard from Illinois State. I did, too.

I was in my third year as Bulls GM then, a position I had taken after serving as the Sixers' business manager in 1968-69. So I called Jack and offered center Clifford Ray and guard Bob Weiss for the pick. Jack politely declined, and the Sixers took Collins.

HELPING HAND

Two years later, I was back in Philadelphia as the general manager. That also happened to be the year the *Daily News* made Phil Jasner its 76ers beat writer. One of the first things the 32-year-old Jasner did was visit our offices to collect his credentials and reference materials. And one of the first people he met was Jack.

"Stick with me, kid," he told Phil, "and I'll teach you the league."

And he did that. He did that for all the writers. Shirk said Jack "taught [him] more about basketball than anybody."

He told them where to stay on the road, where to find a cup of coffee (or something stronger) after a game, what the best shortcut might be to each arena: basic survival techniques.

When we hired Billy early in the '77-78 season, he found that Jack was more than a friend; he was a mentor and a teacher, someone who "cared about me as a person," Cunningham said.

An avid reader, McMahon would often give Billy books he thought he might like. And Jack always had a story to tell. He might repeat himself every now and then, but Billy never tired of listening to him. "He was a great Irishman," Billy said.

Billy can recall only one time where he grew angry at Jack. We were in Chicago getting pounded by the Bulls when the alarm went off on Jack's wristwatch. Billy exploded, "even though," he said years later, "it was funny."

Jack never wore that watch on the bench again.

One time both of them were in a bar in Atlanta after a loss to the Hawks, when a guy came up to Billy and started making racially charged comments about some of the players. But before Billy could go after the guy—and he was fully prepared to do that—Jack jumped in.

"You can't get in a fight," he told Billy. "I can get in a fight."

So Billy ended up dragging Jack out of the place.

The players called him "Uncle Jack" or, when his nose flushed after an adult beverage or two, "Jack O'Lantern."

"Every guy on the team loved him because they were comfortable and confident with him," Billy said. "They'd tell Jack things they'd never share with me. But Jack wasn't a pushover with the players. He'd tell them the truth even if it was painful, and would never sugarcoat his answers."

In fact, Billy said, "Jack had the ability to tell you to your face you were a real so-and-so, and you'd smile and say, 'Thank you.'"

It reached a point where Billy wouldn't have to talk to a player when a problem arose. Jack would take it upon himself to pull the guy aside and smooth the waters.

"They understood [him]," Billy said, "and responded."

AL

Al Domenico, our veteran trainer, was not quite as sentimental about the guys we cut as Jack McMahon. The minute someone was traded or waived, it was, "Off with their heads."

Maybe that warrants further explanation.

On one wall in the trainer's room were team pictures from all the teams Al had served, dating back to 1964-65, the year the NBA mandated that every club have its own full-time trainer. The odd thing about all these team pictures was that every player's head was missing, having been removed by Al.

The head was then moved to a bulletin board elsewhere in the room, meaning you had the ghoulish spectacle of headless team pictures on one wall, and disembodied heads on another.

Al did not recall (or, at least, would not say) why he did this when he was asked in 2006. The best explanation, perhaps, came courtesy of Franklin Edwards: "That was Al. . . . Al Domenico was one of a kind."

We had a few of those. Besides Al, there was Dave Zinkoff, our public address announcer. And there was Harvey Pollack, our public relations guy: The Zink and Superstat, respectively.

Both had been part of the league for as long as there had been a league. And both were, shall we say, quirky.

Al, a Northeast Philly guy, hadn't been around quite as long as either Harvey or The Zink. But he had been around long enough. He had also been around the block a few times, having served in the Marine Corps, and then as a trainer in roller derby and professional wrestling before winding up in hoops.

Along the way, he played the ponies, played angles, played with people's minds. No one was spared. Not the unsuspecting fringe player who showed up at rookie camp in the summer only to be told by Domencio that, gee, he sure didn't have his name on his roster.

Opponents weren't spared, either; Al was one of the league's foremost bench jockeys, and he took particular delight in needling Larry Bird. Liked to call him "Harelip," because of his wispy mustache. (Bird, deciding he had had enough one time, veered out of the pregame layup line and headed straight for Al. Steve Mix saw what was happening and blocked Bird's path. But as Al recalled, "Nothing was going to happen.")

Nor was Harold Katz spared Al's wiles. When Harold asked about Moses

Malone's weight—one of Katz's favorite topics—Al would give him an acceptable figure, a figure he'd arrived at after asking Moses, "What do you want to weigh today?"

"Moses and I came up with all sorts of elaborate plans to work around those [weight] issues," Domenico said. "You've got to keep the superstar happy."

There are those like Darryl Dawkins who claim Al went a little too far to provide for the marquee players. Dawkins swears he was hurt one time during a game, and looked up to see Al rushing to his aid. But then, Dawkins claims, Al continued past him to tend to Julius Erving, who was also injured.

Domenico dismissed that as "one of Darryl's stories."

Al had a few of his own, some of them quite believable.

THE ZINK

Dave Zinkoff was never out of character.

"How ya doin', Zink?" someone might ask.

"Never better," he would respond—only it would come out, "Nev-AH bet-TAH."

He delighted in making sure that everyone else felt the same about themselves. In private moments, he would present salamis—yes, salamis— to friends, to players who gave good performances (including opponents), and to strangers who did good deeds.

And his noisier alter ego was a one-man sideshow, a mischievous soul who managed to amuse and entertain crowds, all in a nasally voice that called to mind gravel rolling around in a cement mixer.

Early arrivals to the Spectrum were informed that smoking was "NOT PERMITTED." But if patrons insisted on doing so, The Zink asked one favor: "PLEASE DO NOT EXHALE."

As the game unfolded and the action heated up, paying customers were treated to the Zink's signature calls. The same man who dubbed a basket by La Salle All-American Tom Gola a "Gola Goal" in the '50s and a slam by Wilt Chamberlain a "Dipper Dunk" in the '60s now heralded a basket by Julius Erving with a cry of, "ERRR-VING."

If the Sixers went on a run, he would announce that the visitors had called "TIMMME" with just the right amounts of glee and derision, as if to ask, "You guys having a little trouble over there?" And as the time ran down he would scream that there were "TWOOO MINUTES LEFT IN THIS BALLGAME," a call that led an *Inquirer* reporter named Edgar Williams to write that The Zink gave fans "a shivery feeling that Armageddon just might be at hand."

Retired NBA forward Mychal Thompson recalled that Zink was "the greatest PA man of all time." Even visiting players imitated him. Boston's Cedric Maxwell and M.L. Carr would do so during warm-ups before some of those grim Celtics-Sixers battles; they just marched over to the scorer's table and mimicked The Zink as he was doing his spiel. And it was said that Cazzie Russell, who played for four teams over 12 seasons, did the best Zink of all.

But there was only one. Dozens of poor imitations came along later and are with us still. But they are little more than high-decibel loudmouths; few can match The Zink's showmanship, wit, and ability to turn a phrase.

SUPERSTAT

The Sixers-Celtics rivalry was such that it was contested not only on the court, but also on the stat sheet.

One time Harvey was in Boston Garden, charting each rebound by Wilt Chamberlain and Bill Russell back when both centers were in their heyday. At game's end, Harvey approached the Celtics' stat guy to compare notes.

The guy told him he had 35 boards for Russell, 23 for Wilt. Harvey had it the other way around.

They argued for a while and were overheard by a writer from *Sports Illustrated*. Sure enough, the next issue of *SI* had a story noting that Boston has been accused of padding Russell's stats.

Red Auerbach was not pleased.

"Any time we played the Celtics after that," Harvey recalled in 2006, "he wouldn't even go near me."

That changed several years later, when Boston's Dave Cowens was battling Washington's Wes Unseld for the rebounding title.

On the season's final day, the Celtics played earlier than the Bullets. Cowens had a decent day on the boards, but Unseld, playing at home, was credited with a season-high 30 rebounds, allowing him to edge out his Boston counterpart.

Pollack questioned that in interviews, and Auerbach took note.

"So the next time I saw him after that article, he walked up to me and shook my hand, and handed me a cigar," Harvey said. "And for the rest of the time that he was the coach, he always gave me cigars, every year. Win or lose, he would give me a cigar."

Harvey's work would often be celebrated. He kept track of blocked shots and dunks long before the league did, and his media guide was a treasure trove of information.

Need to know the league leaders in technical fouls? That was in there. Need to know a player's little-known first name? So was that. Need to know the nickname of each of Darryl Dawkins' dunks (e.g., "Sexophonic Turbo Delight")? That was there, too.

Harvey, another Philly guy, wasn't actually our full-time publicist until 1980, though he liked to say that for years he did a part-time job full-time. Along the way he had his hand in some milestone moments, none bigger than Wilt Chamberlain's 100-point game on March 2, 1962, in Hershey, Pennsylvania.

When a wire-service photographer came looking for a shot of Wilt in the locker room after the game, it was Harvey who scrawled "100" on a sheet of paper and handed it to Wilt. Wilt held it up, the photographer snapped, and it became one of the most well-known photos ever.

Harvey overlapped the Wilt Era and the Doc Era (not to mention the Charles Barkley and Allen Iverson Eras). He also served as the publicity director for the Philadelphia Department of Recreation. He kept the stats at various college games and wrote columns about the Eagles, Phillies (under the pseudonym "Curly Diamond"), and boxing (as "K.O. Battle") for a weekly newspaper called the *Guide*. He also reviewed movies and shows for various suburban publications.

"He was always getting stuff on the cuff," *Inquirer* columnist Bill Lyon said. "He never paid for a dinner or a movie in his life. Sometimes it was like he was America's Guest."

Which raises the possibility of a new category for the media guide: "Most Freebies, Lifetime."

10

Every game, it seemed, was the same.

The ones in the Spectrum would begin with The Zink quickly introducing the visitors' starters, then pausing briefly before bellowing, "AND NOWWWWW, YOUR SIXER STARTERS."

Only it would come out, in Zink-speak, as "YOAH SIX-AH STAH-TAHS."

And away he would go: "West Texas State, No. 10, Mo Cheeks." But it always sounded like a single word: "WestTexasStateNo.10MoCHEEKS."

Cheeks would come out to the foul line, head bowed, careful to avoid looking into the camera the cable-TV guy trained on him.

Next was Andrew Toney ("SouthwestLouisianaNo.22AndrewTONNN-EEE"). Toney would jog out, with his head held high and his chest puffed out, looking bulletproof.

Then, Moses Malone ("PetersburgHighSchoolNo.2centermanMoses-MAL-ONNNE"). Malone's gait was almost grandfatherly, his face expressionless, a blank slate.

Next was Marc Iavaroni ("VirginiaNo.8MarcEye-VARONI"). Happy to be here. Happy to be anywhere.

And finally, Julius Erving. The intro was The Zink's pièce de résistance, one that would resonate with fans for years to come: "MassachusettsNo.6JuliusERRRRRR-VING." The Doctor, rising from the bench, would clap his hands once, smile, and then gather with the others.

Every game would also start with the Sixers running the same play. Billy

Cunningham remembers it as the "fist" play. Matty Guokas doesn't recall that it had an official name, only that it came to be known as "Motion for Andrew"—even though there was very little motion. Toney would pinball his guy off a screen or two, then wind up with a jumper on the left baseline, one he would bury with regularity.

"If we ran it 80 times," Guokas said, "Andrew scored on 60 of them."

It's not uncommon for an NBA team to begin a game with the same play—perhaps, Billy suggested, out of superstition. "You know how coaches are," he said.

Still, Chuck Daly, who began that season coaching the hapless Cleveland Cavaliers (and ended it doing TV work for the Sixers), found it "mind-boggling" that Cunningham would always start off this way.

"If I was the other coach, I'd go knock [Toney] down," Daly said. "Anything to stop the play."

Which actually became the favored defensive approach of the Detroit Pistons teams Daly later coached to two championships.

The Sixers never ran this play the rest of the night, which to Guokas was curious: Why not use it more often? If it worked at the beginning of the first quarter, shouldn't it work midway through the third?

But in Billy's mind, once was enough. And he always made clear what he wanted, going so far as to diagram the play in the pregame huddle—before every game.

"I used to chuckle," Guokas said. "Game 57, and Billy drew it up like we'd never ran it before."

FAMILIAR ENDING

The games started the same, and usually ended the same, too. We won our first six. Not to mention 10 of our first 11, 20 of our first 24, and 34 of our first 39. From there we moved to 50-7, the best start in NBA history to that point, before finally topping out at 57-9.

The biggest constant of all was Moses.

"He'd go to the basket, go to the basket, go to the basket," said Mark Eaton, the Utah Jazz's mountainous 7-foot-5 center. "He never let up on you."

"Moses didn't allow bad nights," said referee Ed T. Rush.

Had those Sixers been a band, Moses would have been the drummer, sitting in the back and providing a steady, unwavering beat. And as he did so, someone else—often Erving or Toney, but sometimes another player—would perform a dazzling solo.

Sonny Hill, the longtime Philadelphia playground impresario, said Malone was more like James Brown, the Godfather of Soul. "He was the hardest-working man in the game," Hill said.

Others had their own metaphors. Eddie Doucette, then a broadcaster for the Bucks, said, "Moses was the Clydesdale that pulled the wagon." But even that seemed inadequate. Clint Richardson said, "Moses was like a hurricane. It was total destruction if anything got in his way."

AUSPICIOUS START

Malone began the season with a 21-point, 17-rebound game against the Knicks in Madison Square Garden, a performance that would become commonplace.

The first real test for him and the team came when the Celtics visited the Spectrum five games into the season. These matchups, like those against the Lakers, were fraught with meaning no matter when they occurred. They provided a measuring stick and determined where each team stood in the championship pecking order. And because of that, they were played with unusual ferocity.

Art Thiel, then a columnist for the *Seattle Post-Intelligencer*, said this three-way steel-cage match was "the acme of basketball rivalries in NBA history."

"Those colorful players and epic, dramatic matchups will never be matched," he said. "There has been nothing like it since."

The stands were always packed, as was press row; the major dailies would send two or three columnists in addition to their beat guys.

When the game was in our building, we always trotted out Grover Washington Jr.—identified by The Zink as a "super saxman"—to perform the national anthem, a soulful rendition that electrified the atmosphere even more. Then they would play, and they would play for keeps.

That was right up Moses' alley, of course. The first time out against Boston with his new club, he played 56 of a possible 58 minutes in a double-overtime thriller. He scored 28 points, snared 19 rebounds, and loosened a few molars.

In the closing seconds of the second extra period, Moses and guard Franklin Edwards engulfed Quinn Buckner in a double-team, resulting in a turnover and a clinching free throw for Frank.

Afterward Boston coach Bill Fitch tried to downplay Moses' game, telling reporters that Darryl Dawkins had always played well against the Celtics, too.

"The difference is, Moses is going to play that way 82 times, so all the other teams are going to feel it a lot more than we will," Fitch said. "It can't be any tougher to beat Philly because Moses is here, because it was already tough as hell."

But everybody knew things were different: the Sixers could match up with the Celtics' talented big men. One of them, Kevin McHale, recalled that the Sixers "had a different attitude with Moses."

"He gave them an inside presence and stabilized them in the middle," McHale said. "They couldn't do that before, with Dawkins and Caldwell Jones. Before Moses, the Sixers had to beat you from outside primarily. But after Moses arrived, they were so much more secure."

Boston forward Cedric Maxwell said it was "a before-and-after thing. Caldwell Jones had given the 76ers an inside defensive presence, and Darryl Dawkins had his moments. When Moses got there, the team finally had a dominating inside player."

BEAT L-A

In early December, Moses scored 29 and collected 14 boards against the Lakers in Los Angeles. Particularly telling were the three offensive rebounds he converted into baskets down the stretch.

"Broke their backs," Billy Cunningham told reporters afterward.

Kareem Abdul-Jabbar? He had 15 points and two rebounds.

"I'm always the most optimistic guy in our locker room," Jack McMahon told the *Daily News'* Phil Jasner, "and seeing this performance makes me believe we're right there again, with a chance to win the whole thing. I know I always feel that way, but this time I feel a little better than I usually do. I mean, I've seen Kareem so many times, and we've never had anybody who could neutralize him. Now we do."

One columnist wrote that Moses Malone, working here against the Phoenix Suns' Larry Nance, didn't get tired—but he was a carrier. *Philadelphia Daily News/Michael Mercanti*

He did more than neutralize Abdul-Jabbar. "Moses just devoured him," said Don Benevento of the *Camden Courier-Post.* Looking back, Benevento finds it hard to believe that any single acquisition has ever worked out better. "They got exactly the guy they needed at exactly the right time," he said.

Our players were reaching the same conclusion after that game against the Lakers. It allowed us to complete a 3-1 road trip and raise our record to 16-3.

"We had made some major trades, and the team was shaken by that," Cunningham said. "They'd lost some good friends, but on that trip they began to understand what Moses had brought to the whole deal and what he could do for them."

Especially since he did it every single night.

MOSES THE METRONOME

On and on Moses went: 24 points and 20 rebounds as we ended a six-game, 11-day road trip with a February 6 victory in Seattle; 23 and 10 in a February 23 rout of Dallas, after returning from the bedside of his mother, who had suffered a mild stroke ("I can't let it get me down when it's time to go to work," he told reporters); 24 and 12 in a March 13 victory over Washington, the team's second in as many nights over the rugged Bullets.

Beating them, Moses told reporters, was "like trying to kill two bulls, then having to fight the matador, too."

But facing Moses was like getting caught in a stampede: "He wasn't flashy, just relentless," said Sixers radio/TV voice Neil Funk, who later in his career would call Chicago Bulls games. "I don't know if I've ever seen a player that relentless. Maybe Michael [Jordan]."

But up to that point, Malone was unparalleled.

"Moses doesn't get tired," *Daily News* columnist Mark Whicker wrote after a December 21 victory over Boston, "but he's a carrier."

"I hated playing against him because he was always trying to create body contact to draw the foul, along with the basket," recalled Eaton, who was seven inches taller than Moses. "Moses might give you 12 head fakes to get you off-balance. Then he'd lean into you to draw the foul. . . . I needed about six inches of space as a shot-blocker to get the right angle. Moses would soak that space right up and make it impossible for me to get at his shot."

Moses was so relentless, said former Pistons center Kent Benson, "it was like trying to guard an octopus." There was "nothing orthodox" about him, said one-time Kansas City Kings big man Steve Johnson. Which perhaps explains why Johnson fouled out in nine minutes while attempting to play Moses one night in 1981-82, Johnson's rookie year.

Milwaukee center Paul Mokeski viewed Moses as "one of the most effective post players ever" because of his versatility and unpredictability. He might shoot a hookshot, or a fadeaway jumper, or, just as likely, he would "bounce it off the board and stick it back in," Mokeski said.

John Lucas, a point guard who played with and against Moses, is certain there were times Malone missed on purpose. Others have made the same claim. But in an interview for this book, Moses swore that was "never" the case.

"Unfortunately, I'd miss them anyway sometimes," he said. "I'd never want to embarrass an opponent and make him look bad. I'd rather make the first one, so I wouldn't have to get the ball and try to make the second one."

But he regularly came up with the second one. And even though he was the aggressor more often than not, he received the benefit of the doubt from referees.

"Darryl Dawkins could have been a much better player, but he never got respect from the officials. Moses got respect to the Nth degree," said Jack McCaffery, then a reporter for the *Trenton Times*.

Especially that year. "He was at the peak of his career and seemed to get every call," Denver center Danny Schayes said. "I remember one time he grabbed me around the neck and threw me down—and I got called for the foul."

OFFICIALLY SPEAKING

The refs gave Moses respect, but they were also amused by him. He called Jake O'Donnell "Jack," and Jack Madden "Jake." Madden, as a result, started calling Moses "Wilt."

"He never asked me why," Madden said.

Another time, Joey Crawford ruled that Moses had stepped on the baseline while making a move in a game against Dallas. Moses began barking at him, but Crawford couldn't understand a word he was saying.

Crawford approached Julius, who was laughing, and asked him to translate. "Moses said, 'Oughta put a beeper on that line,'" Doc said.

Not long after that, a survey came out listing Crawford among the league's top ten officials. The next time he worked a Sixers game, he called a loose-ball foul on Moses.

"That ain't no top-ten call," Moses screamed.

THE UNREACHABLE STAR

To many people, Moses was hard to reach and harder to read.

"Billy didn't know what to make of Moses Malone," Matt Guokas said. "He was so quiet and hardly spoke. He was coachable, but we never knew if we were getting through to him. As the season started, Billy said to me one day, 'When the big fella's playing, we're real good.' That was the understatement of the year."

If Billy couldn't reach him, reporters were seldom allowed within his stratosphere.

"Moses was difficult," *Daily News* columnist Ray Didinger said. "He was the opposite of Doc. He didn't care about publicity. He didn't care about helping you do your job. We weren't on his radar."

That wasn't completely the case. Two years after the championship season, *Daily News* columnist Stan Hochman ripped the irrepressible Charles Barkley, and Barkley was fuming in the locker room at St. Joseph's University, where we practiced. Who in creation was Stan Hochman?

Malone, seated nearby, looked up and said, "Older guy. Got gray hair. Got long sideburns. Never know where the guy is coming from [with his questions]." It was an exact description.

"I really enjoyed covering him," Phil Jasner said years later. "He wanted you to be leery. But if you challenged him, he would answer your question."

Not always, though. Didinger was asked to do a long feature story on Moses late in the season. He did the legwork, talked to all the secondary sources, but still had to speak with Malone.

Moses would not do the interview even though his agent, Lee Fentress, intervened on Didinger's behalf, as did Cunningham and Katz. So Jasner suggested that Didinger go with us on a road trip, grab five minutes with Malone here and there. Didinger did, only to learn that Malone wouldn't speak after practice. Nor in Milwaukee. Nor on Thursdays.

The road trip continued, but Didinger called his editor and told him he was going no further. "I'm wasting my time and your money by doing this," he told him.

So he came home and wrote a story entitled "Moses Makes His Private Life Most Valuable." In it, he detailed how Moses grew up fatherless in a tough neighborhood in Petersburg, Virginia, called the Heights; how his mom, Mary, worked two jobs to make ends meet; how Moses honed his game on the courts of a Virginia Avenue schoolyard, often during solitary late-night sessions.

Didinger reported that Moses was an immediate star in high school for a team that went 50-0 and won a state title each of Malone's last two years.

His recruitment was a circus. College coaches camped out in Petersburg for months on end. Moses made 24 campus visits; after the one to Oral Roberts, the school's founder promised to cure Mary Malone's ulcers if only her son would matriculate.

Moses ultimately committed to Maryland, but things remained tenuous for the Terrapins—especially after he played on their entry in the Urban Coalition League, a summer league in Washington, D.C. One night he would face some of the Washington Bullets' fringe players. Another he would face some top-flight college guys. And every night Moses more than held his own, leading everyone to believe the whispers were true about him making the prep-to-pro leap.

"I don't think they were whispers," future Terrapin (and longtime NBA guard) Brad Davis recalled early in 2007. "I think it was pretty loud. Everybody knew if he wanted to [turn pro], he could. We were trying to keep him at Maryland, but it didn't work out."

Moses' mom, Didinger wrote, was no more enthused about the idea of her son skipping college. But he ultimately signed a seven-year, $3 million contract with the ABA's Utah Stars and never looked back. (The Terps were another matter. Led by their three-headed backcourt of John Lucas, Mo Howard, and Davis, they fell a game short of the Final Four in '74-75.)

Looking back, Didinger called his pursuit of Malone "one of the strangest journalistic odysseys I've ever been involved in." But he earned an award in a state-wide writing competition for the story.

"I guess that tells you interviews are overrated," he said.

Moses did consent to a long interview with *Playboy* magazine the summer after we won the championship, one for which he was reportedly paid $40,000. In it he said he had no interest in speaking to reporters, "because they're gonna write what they want to write, so let 'em write what they want to write."

The net effect of Malone's arm's-length dealings with the media is that he became "the least publicized true superstar in the history of the league," in the estimation of Neil Funk.

BEHIND CLOSED DOORS

Although Moses wasn't interested in talking to reporters, that wasn't the case when it came to his teammates.

"Everybody loved Moses," Mitchell Anderson said. Marc Iavaroni said that Malone was "the team entertainer." Moses was the guy who called backup center Mark McNamara "Tank," after the comic-strip character, the guy who joked that the rented Dodge Colt driven by John Kilbourne, our strength and flexibility coach, was "a Matchbox car," the guy who gave Andrew Toney constant grief about his wardrobe.

"Moses was a really funny guy," said Al Domenico, then the Sixers' trainer. "Still is."

Shielding his sense of humor from the public at large was entirely calculated. McNamara, who immediately grew close to Malone because they played the same position, realized that from day one.

"He was super sharp," Mark said. "People didn't understand him because he didn't want to be understood."

"If you knew him," Domenico said, "you had to love him. He was a funny, funny man."

But only those in the locker room really knew him, And in different ways, too.

CREATURE OF HABIT

On the road, Moses would usually have breakfast with guards Clint Richardson and Maurice Cheeks. "We just ate," Richardson said. "There wasn't much conversation."

Moses didn't remember it quite that way. He remembered that Maurice would order pancakes and bacon, without fail. "I'd ask him to let me have one of his pancakes," Moses said, "but he'd never give me one."

Lunch was usually on Kilbourne. His background was in dance, but he always agreed to square off against Moses in a post-practice shooting contest, with the loser—guess who?—buying. Never mind that Kilbourne was making $25,000 a year while Moses was making over $2 million.

Kilbourne enjoyed Moses' company and his constant teasing. One day, Kilbourne got a little payback.

Moses' important mail was supposed to go to his agent, but on occasion it would get mixed in with all his fan mail. And the way Kilbourne remembers it, "Oftentimes he just threw it away."

Kilbourne decided to sort through the pile one day, just to see if Malone might have disposed of something important. He came upon an envelope from the league office, and opening it found Moses' All-Star Game check. It was for about $3,000.

"That gave me something to tease him about," Kilbourne said, "because he was always teasing me."

It was no different where the rookies were concerned. "He talked about us," Mitchell Anderson said of Moses, "and he talked to us."

He had them run errands for him, Anderson said. But there were also times when he would pick up the tab for them at dinner. Or if he were going out on the town, he'd invite them along.

Some days the other veterans would be allowed to sit out practice. Moses never would, and he would engage in spirited scrimmages against the rookies, talking trash and banging bodies.

"He [was] playing for real," Russ Schoene said. "Those practices were a kick. . . . He wouldn't give up a layup in practice. He'd try to take you in practice and dunk on you. Talking trash to Moses was the highlight of our day."

11

As Moses' first season unfolded, the rest of the league quickly came to understand that this was a team not only of uncommon talent, but of uncommon resolve.

"You could see the fire in their eyes," said Lakers general manager Jerry West, himself a fierce competitor during his Hall of Fame playing career.

Jack McCaffery, then with the *Trenton Times*, saw the same thing. He saw a team that took on Julius Erving's late-game persona for an entire season.

"Late in the game, he seemed to have a different face," McCaffery said. "He went into another personality. He didn't have to say he wanted the ball; he gave a walk and a little sneer, which meant: 'Give me the ball. I'm going to find a way for us to win.' . . . He went from someone who was enjoying the game to almost anger. The '83 year was an entire year of that, an entire year of Doc's look."

Certainly Moses gave all our players great confidence. Certainly they knew that they might not ever have another opportunity like this. And the other thing, McCaffery said, was, "They had had enough. They had failed enough and they weren't going to fail again. You don't see that from many teams. All the failures prior to that gave that team a resolve that it wasn't going to be beaten."

Jim Foster, the St. Joseph's women's basketball coach, believed that the launch point for the 1982-83 team had come not on the day Moses was signed, but on the day we marched into Boston Garden and beat the Celtics in Game 7 of the 1982 Eastern Conference finals.

"Nobody in the city of Philadelphia gave the Sixers a chance in that game," he said. "I think that win in Game 7 on the road laid the foundation for the success in 1983."

McCaffery said, "It wasn't a stand-alone team. It was the result of the teams that came before it. It was a culmination. . . . You never saw Doc take his eyes off the ball that year. Time was running out, and that was his best chance to win one. I don't remember a team playing with more confidence than that, ever."

If there were lapses, they were only momentary. In the playoffs that year, *Daily News* columnist Ray Didinger remembers seeing Doc hesitate to chase a loose ball. That drew an instant response from Billy Cunningham.

"Doc," he screamed from the bench, "do you want it?" For a moment, Didinger recalled, Julius looked quizzical. "Then go get it," Billy yelled.

It was one of the few times anybody needed a reminder.

THE VIEW FROM THE PRESS BOX

Not everyone was captivated by what the '82-83 team was doing. *Inquirer* beat writer George Shirk, for one, thought it was a boring season. There was no real news, no real intrigue.

The *Daily News'* Phil Jasner, on the other hand, said it was fascinating to chronicle a team on such a crusade, such a night-in, night-out mission.

That they held such divergent views is not surprising, since they were, in Shirk's view, an "odd couple." They got along well. They traveled together and exchanged ideas. But they were as different as could be.

Jasner was older and more serious, and he had been covering the team since the 1972-73 season. Shirk was younger and more irreverent. He had come on the beat in '81-82 after the *Inquirer* hired him away from the *Des Moines Register* in his native Iowa.

Their differences did not end there. "He'd explain Passover to me," Shirk said wryly, "and I'd explain Easter to him."

Shirk's musical tastes ran toward punk bands like the Clash. The day Moses Malone arrived in town, Jasner went from the news conference to a Neil Diamond concert in the Spectrum, then went home and wrote his story for the *Daily News'* forgiving deadline.

"Great concert," he remembered. "Tremendous. 'Cracklin' Rosie.'"

It's no surprise, then, that they view that season as they do.

"It was a crummy team to cover—in retrospect, even more so," Shirk recalled. "As a newspaperman, what you want ideally is a team that overachieves."

The Sixers only achieved—albeit at a very high level. "In '83 the 76ers were on a march to the championship from the day they broke training camp," Shirk said. "That storyline never broke. Every day they were blowing away teams. There was no drama at all."

But Jasner was fascinated by the team's sustained excellence and by its crusading mentality. "I enjoyed every bit of that season," he said. "I'm sure that there were negative moments, and there were moments when somebody was mad at somebody, and somebody said something controversial, and all of that. . . . But that team was on a mission. That team was out to do something."

AUSPICIOUS DEBUT

Bobby Jones fouled out in overtime of the season's first meeting with the Celtics, and Billy Cunningham looked down his bench for a potential replacement. No longer did he see veterans Steve Mix or Mike Bantom. Instead, he saw two rookies, Marc Iavaroni and Russ Schoene.

He chose Schoene, and Russ—the second of our second-round draft picks—rewarded him by making a jumper in the lane with 1:07 left in the second overtime, putting us ahead by a point.

Then the kid began to contribute regularly. He scored 25 points against Milwaukee. He shot 6-for-6 and 6-for-9 in consecutive games. He grabbed a big offensive rebound late in a victory over Phoenix. Nobody could believe it, least of all him.

"It came fast, and I want to say too soon," he remembered. "I wasn't thinking; I was just playing. . . . It still amazes me I was making a contribution on that good a team. Certainly I expected to play well; I was always mad when I didn't play well. The reason I was so successful was that I wasn't thinking about it."

We had used the 45th overall pick on Schoene after getting a heads-up from my old classmate at Wake Forest, CBS-TV college basketball analyst Billy Packer. Billy had seen Russ playing for Tennessee-Chattanooga in the NCAA Tournament in an upset of North Carolina State and a near-upset of Minnesota, and he'd liked his size (6-foot-10) and skill set.

Growing up on a farm in Trenton, Illinois, he would shoot around on a basket moored at the end of a 15-foot-wide concrete slab left behind when some structure or other was torn down. But he didn't really get serious about basketball until he shot up to 6-foot-6 in high school, and even then he attracted little recruiting interest; he wound up at Mineral (Missouri) Junior College, then at Tennessee-Chattanooga.

If all that wasn't enough to make his head spin, there was more once he made the team. The Sixers were on a flight somewhere during the preseason or early in the regular season when Julius Erving beckoned for Russ to sit next to him.

Doc started out by offering "the general pep talk to a young kid," Schoene recalled, then said something that nearly floored the rookie—that Russ "reminded him of himself, in a certain way."

"That kind of blew me away," Schoene said. "Quite honestly, I don't remember the next five minutes of what he said. It was like, 'What? How in the world could I ever remind him of himself?' It was pretty uplifting. It gave me kind of a spring in my step."

At the other extreme was Billy Cunningham. The Sixers were playing Washington when Russ tried to box out Jeff Ruland, the Bullets' burly center, as one of Ruland's teammates was shooting a free throw. Ruland buried a forearm in the rookie's back, nearly driving him over the baseline.

Whistle. Foul on Schoene.

Billy called a timeout, most of which he spent chewing out Russ. "He was telling me he was sending me to the Eastern League," Schoene said. "I'd never heard of it. I think it was out of business." (It was. By that point, it was called the Continental Basketball Association.)

"That was one of those things," Matty Guokas said. "Russ was a rookie and very wide-eyed. He was trying to soak it all in and learn. He would look you in the eye. Unfortunately guys like that become whipping boys. Other guys, you can't jump on them, because they sulk or you don't know what else."

Billy was well aware of this, having experienced the same sort of treatment when he was a rookie in 1965-66. Hardly wide-eyed, he enjoyed a big year off the bench. But after lighting it up in the first half of a game against the Knicks, coach Dolph Schayes stormed into the locker room and lit into Billy and fellow rookie Gerry Ward.

Cunningham was thoroughly confused. He had played well, and Ward had hardly played at all. But Schayes went on and on about how they weren't helping the team.

As the team made its way back onto the court, Schayes—once a great player, and a prince of a guy—pulled Billy aside and apologized.

"I had no one else to yell at," Dolph told him.

It was much the same thing the following year, when Alex Hannum replaced Schayes and coached the Sixers to a championship.

"At halftime, just to get everybody's attention, one [out] of every three games, two [out] of every three games, he would go off," Guokas, a rookie guard on that team, recalled. "It was always general comments. He generally meant Wilt. He and Wilt didn't speak."

But on and on Hannum would go: We have to defend better. We have to rebound better. And so forth. Sometimes power forward Luke Jackson would look at Hannum and ask, "What's this 'we' stuff?"

When he became a coach, Billy was generally straightforward; if he had a problem with a player, he let him know about it.

"There were times I would dance a little bit," he said, "but not too much."

TONEY TIME

The play was supposed to be "Two-Up for Moses." That's what Billy drew up, anyway.

Seconds remained in overtime of the January 5 game against the Lakers in the Spectrum, a sparkling Sunday afternoon affair between the defending champions and the champions-to-be. Kareem Abdul-Jabbar didn't play because of a migraine, but Magic Johnson generated a triple-double: 23 points, 20 assists, 12 rebounds. Jamaal Wilkes scored 36 points. Moses shrugged off a muscle pull in his back to pile up 21 points and 15 rebounds.

Julius scored 27, two on a majestic windmill dunk that saw him swoop in from the left wing on the break and soar over Michael Cooper. Cazzie Russell, the ex-NBA player who was then coaching in the CBA, said after watching on television that it looked like Doc left Cooper off at the sixth floor, while he continued up to the eighth.

Cooper, for his part, realized in mid-flight that he wasn't going to be able to challenge the shot, so he ducked under the backboard to avoid hitting his head.

The dunk remains a staple of highlight videos all these years later. But Cooper doesn't mind. "It bothers my kids more so than me," he said.

The slam gave the Sixers a four-point lead with 1:27 left. Memorable as it was, all it did was set the stage for a dramatic ending.

The Lakers came back to tie it, at 120-all.

"Sixers call TIMMME."

In the huddle, Billy settled on "Two-Up for Moses."

The ball was inbounded to Maurice Cheeks, who was supposed to initiate the play.

And that's as far as it went. Andrew Toney commandeered the ball from Maurice near midcourt. Billy, right on cue, sprang from his seat and charged down the sideline. What was Andrew doing?

Cooper, the Lakers, best defender, crouched before him. Toney cradled the ball and sized him up.

It was a familiar scene, one that led *Daily News* columnist Stan Hochman to ask Andrew later in the year, semi-seriously, if he was staring his man down, waiting for him to blink.

"I can't be looking at his eyes," Toney told Hochman. "I got it in my mind to score. I ain't got time to be lookin' at his eyes."

Looking back, Cooper is not the least bit surprised at the way this final play unfolded. "Great players always want the ball," he said.

Especially then. Andrew had scored 10 of his 28 points in the final eight minutes of regulation, and to that point had four more in overtime. He had to ride this out, had to seize the moment.

Finally he attacked, roaring past Cooper and heading for the lane. The Los Angeles defense converged, but as Toney had once told Franklin Edwards, he always took that into account, always worried more about the help than the first line of resistance.

He came to a stop on the left side of the key, 10 feet from the basket, and rose to shoot. James Worthy and Bob McAdoo were there to challenge him, but Andrew managed to kiss his jumper off the glass and in. Five seconds remained.

"Andrew's shot amazed me," Cheeks told reporters after the 122-120 victory. "I don't know how he got it over all those hands."

Toney was, as usual, nonplussed.

"I know I can't make 'em all," he told the media mob, "but I'll never shy away from taking 'em."

CAUGHT WITH HIS PANTS ON

Mitchell Anderson was released on December 20, his brief tenure with the Sixers never having gotten off the ground possibly because he couldn't get his pants off.

Billy tried to insert him in the second quarter of the home opener against New Jersey. But as Anderson ran to the scorer's table, he was unable to unsnap his warm-up pants.

"The last [snap] didn't come off," he said. "I was trying to kick it off, and it got tangled in my shoes."

Play resumed. Billy disgustedly told him to return to the bench.

"I thought I'd go back in," Anderson said years later. "I missed my window of opportunity."

But he did not. Not that night, and not very often after that. He appeared in only 13 of our 25 games before he was waived with an assurance from Cunningham that Utah would sign him—which the Jazz did.

Did his wardrobe malfunction lead to his departure? "I'm not that cruel," Cunningham said.

"Billy was cool," Anderson said. "We all laughed about it later. I was the butt of jokes for a while."

But Earl Cureton thought the incident was "probably about the end for Mitchell." And John Nash said it "possibly accelerated the decision" to let him go.

"The idea was, if you're a kid trying to get a chance to play and the coach calls your number, don't lollygag down to the scorer's table; get your tail down there and get in at the earliest possible opportunity," Nash said. "It's a pretty good life, the NBA life, and whatever it takes to impress the coach—if it means you've got to rip your sweats off to get into a game, rip your sweats off. That's basically what it's all about."

12

The way Bob Ryan saw it, Julius Erving's game had evolved by 1982-83. At age 32 he was "no longer a relentlessly dominant player," the longtime *Boston Globe* columnist said.

Then again, Ryan said, "He didn't still have to be Dr. J. Julius Erving was just fine—a terrific small forward and one of the 10 or 12 best players in the league."

Clark Kellogg, a rookie forward with Indiana that year, agreed that Doc "picked and chose his spots more." He could afford to, given Moses' dominance and Andrew Toney's emergence as a star. But Kellogg said that when the need arose, Doc could still "rise up and get you."

He seemed to do so at the most opportune times, as when he scored 36 points in the home opener against New Jersey, or 44 in a December victory over Detroit, one game after we lost to the Celtics.

There was also a February night in Chicago when Billy Cunningham thought the lowly Bulls were taking the game to us and told the players so at halftime. That prompted a second-half explosion by Julius, en route to a 34-point, eight-rebound, four-block, four-steal performance.

Billy believed Julius was "the most coachable player ever."

"We had a wonderful relationship for eight years," Cunningham said. "He had to listen to all my speeches, over and over."

Billy had been a radio analyst for the Sixers when Julius arrived in 1976. Billy said at that point, Doc "didn't feel it was his team."

"He wouldn't step on people's toes when he first got to Philly," Billy said, "and there were a lot of people at that time, outstanding talents, that also thought they were stars. And you just can't have so many 'stars.'"

Once we revamped the roster, Julius became the unquestioned centerpiece. "Doc wanted the responsibility," Billy said. "He embraced the role of being the star. And there wasn't anybody [who was] envious, which can happen quite often. Everyone was happy that Julius was the star."

Moses' arrival meant he would have to adjust, that there would be times he would play a secondary role. And Erving said when he stepped forward, it was "based on the matchups."

"That year it wasn't about scoring for me," he said, though he averaged 21 points a game. "It was about getting wins, getting home-court advantage in all the playoff series, and getting a championship ring."

DOC'S SHOW

The All-Star Game in Los Angeles was all about the show. Julius would later call his 25-point MVP performance "one of the highlights of [his] career."

He was heartened by the fact that Moses, Andrew Toney, and Maurice Cheeks had joined him on the East's roster, just the fifth time in league history that four teammates had played in the game. And Billy was the coach.

Before the game, Doc exchanged pleasantries with Marvin Gaye, who was about to sing the national anthem. And that, Julius recalled, "really set the stage for a great game. . . . I was loose and the game was like we were out on the playground," he said.

He punctuated his day with five dunks, and afterward the other players could only marvel. Milwaukee's Marques Johnson told reporters that there were times when he was sure Erving had lost a step. Now this. Now one more reminder that Father Time had not yet run Doc down in the open court.

EXCITABLE BOY

Toney was the last of the four Sixers to be named to the All-Star Game; like Cheeks, his friend and backcourt partner, it was the first time he had been chosen. Before the announcement came, Phil Jasner had called the league office and asked for a heads-up, not so much because he wanted a scoop, but because he knew Billy would want to know, and would want to be the one to inform Andrew.

Jasner's request was honored. He passed word on to Billy, then watched as Cunningham told Andrew. Jasner recalled that when Billy relayed the news, "You could see the light shine in Andrew's eyes. He was so excited."

It figured to be the first of many such trips for the young guard.

RANDOM ACTS OF KINDNESS

If Julius' game changed, little else did.

One snowy night in December, we beat the lowly Cleveland Cavaliers in the Spectrum. Longtime Cavaliers radio broadcaster Joe Tait did his postgame show, then headed for the team bus, only to discover that it had left without him.

"I was frantic to get a ride to the hotel," he recalled.

Just about then a car approached. Tait said its dashboard was "lit up like a 747." Doc was the pilot, and at the sight of this forlorn figure he rolled down his window.

"What, did they leave you?" he asked Tait.

Informed that they had, Julius volunteered to drive him through the snowstorm to his hotel. And from that point forward, Tait said, Julius was his "all-time favorite 76er."

That was a widely held view. When we had played in Los Angeles a few weeks earlier, John Kilbourne, our strength and conditioning coach, was driving Doc out of the Forum after practice.

A group of kids gathered around the vehicle. "Do you have anything to do?" Julius asked Kilbourne. Kilbourne said he did not, which wasn't true. He had some family members in California he wanted to visit.

"I'd like to talk to these kids," Doc said. So he climbed out of the car, met with the group, signed autographs, and made their day.

"I saw him do that over and over again," Kilbourne said.

"What stands out to me goes beyond the terrific dunks and the hair that was flying," retired Milwaukee center Bob Lanier said. "What I always tell people about Julius is that he was so humble for a man of such great distinction. He was the first man to come into a room with kids, and the last to leave. He would sign every single autograph for every single kid in the room. That tells me a lot about an athlete, because that's hard to do."

In February of the championship season, Doc had eight dunks in a 24-point game against Dallas. Afterward he talked about all the things that were going on in his life away from the court, how there weren't enough hours in the day to get everything done.

Daily News columnist Stan Hochman asked Bobby Jones about that.

"I don't know how he does it," Bobby told him. "He's always going somewhere. If I tried that, I'd be in the hospital in two weeks."

"Well, at least Julius would come and visit you," Stan said.

"Yeah, and he'd bring flowers, too," Bobby said.

THE QUEST

Despite everything, Doc remained zeroed in on basketball, zeroed in on a season that was becoming more remarkable by the day.

"I just knew something would go wrong," said Bill Livingston, then a columnist for the *Philadelphia Inquirer*. "It always had."

True. It was "We Owe You Five" by that point. And it was beginning to look as though we would never have a better opportunity to repay our debt.

"Like everyone else, I wanted Doc to get a ring," Livingston said. "I had great fondness for the man."

There was no win-it-for-Julius battle cry in the locker room, however.

"He never made you feel like that," Marc Iavaroni said. "It was definitely a 'We' thing."

SILENT PARTNERS

Maurice Cheeks and Bobby Jones hid in plain sight. Every night they provided the same things: the same effort and the same results. It was easy to take them for granted, and given all the stars around them, easy to forget they were there. Which is just how they liked it.

Both shot 54 percent from the field during the '82-83 regular season. Both shot better than 75 percent from the line. Maurice was "the first strand of barbed wire in the Sixers' no-man's-land defense," as *Daily News* columnist Mark Whicker described him, while Bobby "could guard anyone," in the estimation of Hubie Brown, then the Knicks coach.

"Think of all the guys Julius didn't have to guard [because of Bobby's presence]," *Sports Illustrated's* Jack McCallum said. Bobby checked small forwards, power forwards, whomever. And as with everything else, he did so with nary a discouraging word.

"I don't think I've ever seen a guy who complained less than Bobby," said Neil Funk, then a broadcaster for the team.

Clint Richardson followed Bobby off the bench and tried to follow his example.

"He's the quiet one, the worker, nothing fancy," Clint once told the *Daily News*. "Just dribbled up the court, got the job done. Let somebody else be on center stage."

Cheeks might have been more statistically noticeable than Bobby or Clint—he tied Wilt Chamberlain's club record by handing out 21 assists against New Jersey in our home opener, and scored a career-high 32 points against Golden State late in the year (a fact that surprised even him when he was apprised of it years later)—but preferred to remain anonymous, despite everyone's best efforts.

Knowing that one of Maurice's off-court passions was chocolate-chip cookies, *Daily News* columnist Stan Hochman showed up at practice one time with four different brands, and asked Cheeks to do a blind taste test. He got two of the four right.

But mostly, the writers got a crumb or two from Maurice, nothing more. Mostly he hid in plain sight.

GOING UP

Clemon Johnson and the rest of the Indiana Pacers awoke on the morning of February 15, 1983 in a Chicago hotel—just another way station on the road to nowhere for a 15-35 team that had lost four straight.

There would be a morning shootaround, a game against the almost-as-woeful Bulls that night, then another plane ride and another game against the Bulls the next night in Indianapolis.

Johnson, the Pacers backup center, had heard the trade rumors: that he might go to the Lakers or Philadelphia. Not a bad choice—the best team in the West or the best team in East. But rumors tend to be a dime a dozen in the NBA; he would believe it only when he was given official word. So he shrugged off another night on the road, got dressed, and trudged downstairs to the team bus.

Jack McKinney, the Pacers coach, intercepted him. "I've got some bad news," he began. Then he told Johnson he had been traded to the 76ers for Russ Schoene.

"I looked at him and was still waiting for the bad news," Johnson remembered, chuckling.

It had been much the same for Reggie Johnson a day earlier. As the Kansas City Kings' practice ended, coach Cotton Fitzsimmons told the third-year forward we had purchased his contract.

"I wasn't too sad about the situation," Reggie said. He'd liked playing for the Kings. It was a decent team, and he was getting regular minutes. Still, he said, "I didn't waste too much time [packing]. . . . When I was told, I was all excited about going."

GOING DOWN

The trade deadline had been midnight on February 14. When it passed without word of a deal, Russ Schoene called Mark McNamara to tell him he was going to go out and celebrate.

"And he wasn't a wild guy," McNamara said.

Unbeknownst to Russ, we had informed the league late the night before that we were close to making a deal with Indiana and had requested that the deadline be extended.

Which is why Schoene was awakened by a phone call a few hours later and asked to come down to our offices in Veterans Stadium. Billy Cunningham was waiting with the bad news.

"I was sitting there, kind of numb," Russ said. "He told me they did everything not to trade me."

Which was true. We still liked Russ, even though his play had fallen off dramatically after a hot start. But McKinney, the old St. Joseph's coach, had been told by his friends in Philadelphia that Schoene had some ability and had insisted that he be included in the deal.

Schoene returned to his apartment and called McNamara once more. He told him what had happened and asked him to come over.

Downcast, he began digging through his cupboards.

"He had this box full of noodles," McNamara said. "He said, 'Here's my stuff. You can have it.'"

His first night with the Pacers, Schoene was sitting on the bench when he happened to look up at the scoreboard and saw that the Sixers were leading Denver 70-38 at halftime.

"They really miss me, don't they?" he said to the guy next to him.

MISSING-MAN FORMATION

February 18 brought a predictably easy 127-98 victory over Houston in Caldwell Jones' homecoming game. We were 45-7, en route to a title. The Rockets were 10-43, en route to 14-68.

"That one year felt like four years," Caldwell recalled. "I went from winning 60 ballgames a year to losing 60. Any time you're losing, it takes five to 10 years off your life."

Del Harris, then the Houston coach, said it was "the worst year of coaching I have endured." He knew going in that he had little talent, little chance. That was understood. He had received assurances that his job would be safe, but as the losses piled up and some of the veterans began sniping at him in the papers, he realized that all bets were off.

"By the middle of January, no one in the organization was speaking to me, particularly not the owner [Charlie Thomas]," said Harris, who was fired at season's end.

The only light at the end of the tunnel, it seemed, was provided by an oncoming train.

"We'd been thinking, we can get a win if the other team is missing a few players," Caldwell said. "That was really a weight on your head, pushing it down. You would dread going to practice, dread going to shootaround, dread going to the game. You can't wait until it's over. . . . We were counting [down] quarters, counting halves: 'We've got so many quarters left.' That was the longest season."

His friends and former teammates, looking on from afar, could only sympathize. He had always been the ultimate gamer, the ultimate winner. And now he was stuck with this ragtag bunch.

"If there is an unfairness in life, it's that I have a ring from Philadelphia and Caldwell doesn't," Franklin Edwards said. "I remember telling Caldwell that, because he deserved to be there."

Others shared that opinion. That includes Billy Cunningham, who offered Caldwell his championship ring early in the 1983-84 season. C.J., true to his nature, turned it down.

13

The weeks passed. The victories piled up. And the impression we left was an everlasting one.

"I can still see Mo Cheeks with the ball, racing down the middle, with Doc on one wing and Bobby Jones on the other," Marques Johnson, a forward for Milwaukee that year, said in early 2007. "Moses is trailing the play, along with Toney, who is waiting to see what develops. What a scary sight to a defender."

The way Marques saw it, he had "the toughest duty in sports" when the Bucks played us: "I had to guard Dr. J on one end," he said, "and then try to score on Bobby Jones on the other end."

But really, there were no easy nights for anyone. We were too balanced, remembered Wally Walker, a forward with Seattle that season. Too resilient, then-Celtic M.L. Carr said. Too complete, ex-Nugget Danny Schayes recalled. Too cohesive, former Warriors coach Johnny Bach said.

"They attacked inside and outside, and they had a kind of joy that's missing today," said Bach, later an assistant on three championship teams in Chicago. "They played like a bunch of kids on the playground and looked as if they actually enjoyed playing. Billy Cunningham brought that Brooklyn competitive spirit and coached them as a team and not as a bunch of individuals. That's the way all teams should play. The Sixers ran well and competed hard every night. That team played basketball the way it was meant to be played. They were a fun team to watch and brought me a lot of joy as a basketball purist."

"It was one of those perfect storm-type situations," Matty Guokas said. Matty had seen it when he and Billy played for the 1966-67 edition of the Sixers, and now he was seeing it again, a perfect meld of talent and opportunity and motivation.

There were few complaints, and few injuries. As veteran NBA executive Joe Axelson noted, our top seven players missed just 28 games between them, ten by Julius. As a result, all the gears meshed. Our starters shot 51.5 percent from the field, 76.8 percent from the foul line. Moses and Julius both averaged over 20 points a game, and Andrew Toney nearly did so.

"This was a balanced, unselfish team, along the order of the 1970 and 1973 New York Knicks and the 1977 Portland Trailblazers," Axelson said. "They could push it up, walk it up, and stop the other teams when it counted."

And as Axelson said, we did it against immeasurably tougher competition than currently exists. There were only 23 teams then—seven fewer than today.

"Do a reverse fantasy league draft," he said. "Take the least qualified 84 players off of the 2006 rosters and visualize the improvement in the game."

Even so, it was clear we were head and shoulders above the field.

"Every time they walked into the building their attitude was, 'You guys don't have a chance tonight,'" said Lester Conner, a rookie guard with Golden State that year.

It didn't matter which building, either. We were 35-6 at home, 30-11 on the road.

Pistons trainer Mike Abdenour remembered that we always staged the dot race, where two illuminated dots crept across a screen on the Spectrum scoreboard, in the third quarter. He remembered something else, too.

By the time the dot race came around, he said, "The game was over."

MEANWHILE, IN BOSTON...

Celtics coach Billy Fitch told the *Boston Globe* in March that being in second place with a 42-15 record was "like chasing Raquel Welch for 365 days without getting a handshake." But for the most part, the Celtics remained unimpressed by our season-long roll.

We split six games with Boston that year, each team winning on its home court. After they beat us by 26 points in the Garden on December 10—our worst loss of the season—Larry Bird told reporters, "In our minds, we're still the best team in the NBA."

After they ended our 10-game winning streak on March 4, center Robert Parish reminded media types that we still had to "come this way if [we were] going to get there."

"It does a lot for our confidence," Parish added, "especially the way we were playing. . . . I don't think they are that much better than us. Not seven games [in the standings]."

The day before, Celtics icon Red Auerbach couldn't resist a dig when the *Daily News'* Phil Jasner asked about our pursuit of 70 victories.

"They've got the momentum, and they're going after it," Auerbach told Jasner. "I hope they go after it. The more they put out now, the harder it'll be in the playoffs. Somebody can get hurt, too. Unfortunately in basketball, when you get the best record it should mean something, but it doesn't count for much. Who knows that we had the best record the last three years in a row? People just ask, 'How many times did you win all the marbles?'"

The rivalry did strange things to people on both sides. Maurice Cheeks, normally the most even-tempered of souls, dunked on M.L. Carr in our 122-105 victory on December 21, then celebrated by applauding in Carr's face—something even Cheeks had a hard time believing when he was asked about it years later.

But at the time, he told reporters, "It was just something I think I had in me. I had to do it. I got riled up."

And with Boston up 22 points midway through the fourth quarter of that December 10 game, Fitch reinserted Bird, something that could only be interpreted as a rub-it-in gesture.

"I'm glad we don't have to play them every other week," Clint Richardson told the media after the December 21 victory. "We'd get ulcers."

But it seemed certain we were on course for a playoff collision. Wasn't that always the case?

THE NEW C.J.

We had had the Celtics in mind when we traded for Clemon Johnson. We figured we would need him to match up with their manglers—and if not theirs, then somebody else's. Playoff games always tended to be halfcourt brawls. You could never have too much size, too much toughness.

"You can look back and every championship team has a guy like that, who can play two positions on the front line for you, bang, [play] tough, come up with plays when you need them," said Clark Kellogg, then a rookie forward for the Pacers. "Scoring's not their emphasis. They're going to be out there to set the hard screens, make an open shot, get a putback, spell the other big guys, defend. You've just got to have guys like that."

Now we did. And while our other midseason acquisition, Reggie Johnson, played sparingly, Clemon became a regular contributor, a guy who could spell Moses in the middle and Marc Iavaroni at power forward.

"Clemon fit in perfectly with us," Clint Richardson said. "He was an enforcer. . . . Clemon was a nice guy, but he would knock your head off."

As soon as Johnson arrived in February, he could sense "a confidence throughout Philadelphia that this team was going to do it all."

Jack Ramsay had drafted him in Portland five years earlier at the recommendation of Temple's John Chaney, who had coached Johnson in a small-college all-star game after his senior year at Florida A&M. Clemon, tutored by Blazers tough guy Maurice Lucas his rookie year, later moved along to Indiana. But when he heard that we had acquired Moses, he told *Daily News* columnist Mark Whicker that he dreamed of playing for us.

"I went to bed one night and thought, 'I wonder if I should call Billy C. and ask him if I could play for him, even three or four minutes a game,'" Johnson told Whicker after joining us. "Sure enough, it's happened."

If Clemon was at first intimidated by Julius Erving, he got over it in part because, naturally, Doc welcomed him with open arms. If he was "frightened" by Moses Malone, he quickly put that aside. Johnson averaged one rebound every 3.4 minutes for us, a figure that compared favorably with those of the league leaders. He also supplied the requisite toughness, and then some. There was a brawl with Chicago guard Reggie Theus in March that resulted in Clemon being fined $1,000. It also put him in the awkward position of having to explain everything to his three-year-old son. "He understood more than I thought," the elder Johnson told the *Daily News*.

But for the most part, there was no need to apologize. He was just the sort of player we needed.

THIS IS A RECORDING

A sports psychologist named Bob Rotello had made an audio tape for Marc Iavaroni before the season, and Marc referred back to it on occasion, finding it helpful as far as "keeping the game simple, and reminding myself I did belong."

That became harder to remember late in the regular season, because after starting the first 69 games, Iavaroni faded into the background—at times coming off the bench, at times not playing at all.

He continued to review another kind of tape—game tape—and didn't always like what he saw. He continued to record his thoughts on a bedside Dictaphone and didn't always like what he had to say.

There was always something. After the team won in San Diego during the team's first West Coast swing of the season, the players were supposed to travel to Los Angeles for the game against the Lakers two nights later. Normally Iavaroni drove Julius Erving and Maurice Cheeks in one of the luxury cars the team rented. But on this occasion Erving was traveling in a limo provided by the Canadian Broadcasting Company, which was filming a documentary about him.

"Take my luggage to the hotel," he told Iavaroni and Cheeks.

So they did. Only they took it to the hotel in San Diego, thinking Erving would pick it up before heading to L.A. But Erving went straight to Los Angeles, and soon discovered his bags had not made the trip. Which led everyone to one conclusion: The rookie messed up.

"It's not fun being around guys, knowing you're a major contributor to a snafu," Iavaroni said.

There was also the time he showed up for a shootaround at 10:50 because Billy Cunningham had said the session would be "10 to 11." And the time against Portland he put his shorts on backwards, something he discovered when he looked down early in the game and saw that the NBA logo, "instead of being on my right thigh, was on my left [butt]."

Billy forgave his lateness, if only because some veterans made the same mistake. The backwards shorts were another matter. "That's where his head is tonight," Billy had muttered.

Marc had his share of good moments, none better than a 19-point game against Milwaukee in January that included the game-winning free throws with five seconds left. Afterward Marques Johnson could only shake his head at the way his team had been done in by somebody named "Macaroni."

But he had plenty of trying times. He had been manhandled by Sonics forward Lonnie Shelton during a February game in Seattle, but when Iavaroni viewed the game tape, he couldn't even detect a particularly painful kidney shot Shelton had delivered. Iavaroni had no problem hearing himself cry out in agony, though.

In March Marc scuffled with Detroit's Ray Tolbert and Isiah Thomas, and was fined $250. That led Iavaroni to recall that while playing in Italy, an American player named Mel Davis fractured his cheekbone with a punch, prompting the fans to chant, "Devi Morire, Devi Morire"—"He must die."

Billy, concerned that Marc was running out of gas down the stretch, sat him down on some occasions, limited his minutes on others. He also told him to fight the urge to go to the gym and shoot on his off-days.

"When I tell you to take the day off," Cunningham said, "take the day off."

The decision was made on the eve of the playoffs to reinsert Iavaroni into the starting lineup, but Jack McMahon told him to play within himself, that he had a tendency to make easy plays hard.

And everyone believed things would be hard enough.

REDSHIRT YEAR

Mark McNamara played so little, he looked at it as a redshirt season. He saw only 182 minutes of action during the regular season, and exactly two in the playoffs. The suspicion was that he could play—"He's not a stiff," assistant coach Jack McMahon told reporters after one of McNamara's rare appearances—but there was little opportunity for him to prove it.

A natural history major at Cal-Berkeley, he had a fondness for snakes that led me to have one of the reptiles on hand for Mark's introductory press conference after we made him the 22nd overall pick. He didn't appreciate that.

"I considered it unprofessional," McNamara said, looking back. "It was like, 'You're really making my start easy here.'"

Mark had also spent the summer prior to his rookie year working as a costumed stand-in for Chewbaca, a huge hairy creature who appears in *The Empire Strikes Back*, one of the Star Wars films. He had gotten the job through his cousin who, while working on the film, was told its producers needed someone 7 feet tall for a role.

While it turned out we had very little need for Mark's 7 feet, he played some roles for us, too. Elvis Presley, for one. Bob Lanier, for another. Told by the veterans that the rookies would have to sing after dinner one night in training camp, Mark dumped a glass of water on his head, slicked back his hair and launched into a spirited rendition of Elvis' "Heartbreak Hotel." That passed muster not only with the veterans, but several civilians who happened to be seated in the hotel dining room where he performed.

Because he was big (not to mention left-handed), he would also be asked to impersonate Bob Lanier in practice sessions prior to our playoff series against Milwaukee.

But mostly McNamara sat. That led to some amusing moments, like the time we were in Los Angeles and he found himself seated next to a skinny guy with shaggy hair and a British accent. He looked vaguely familiar, but McNamara couldn't place the face until one of the Laker Girls jogged past.

"Hi, Rod," she said. As in Rod Stewart, the rock singer. Stewart told McNamara he didn't really know much about basketball, so Mark spent the night explaining the game to him.

When Mark did play, it was in games we led handily. Which didn't mean it was a low-pressure situation, he recalled. Not when the game was at home, seeing as we had a promotion that rewarded fans with an Egg McMuffin sandwich at McDonald's the following morning if we scored 125 points or more, or limited an opponent to 76 or fewer.

"That was the worst part of the game for us as players," McNamara said, referring to himself and the other deep reserves. "We got in, and we hadn't played in two weeks. The whole crowd is waiting to see if they get their Egg McMuffins. There was more pressure."

We managed to give the fans McMuffins nine times, and we came within five points on six other occasions. One of the successes was a 132-85 rout of Atlanta on December 8, a game in which McNamara corralled seven rebounds in eight minutes.

Afterward, a reporter told him that that projected to 42 rebounds in a 48-minute game. "Thank God for those projections," McNamara said.

That rout was payback for some showboating the Hawks had done while beating us eight days earlier, in Atlanta. It had been just our third loss in 16 games, and as Atlanta star Dominique Wilkins remembered, "We were celebrating like we won the title." Our players did not forget.

"Let's get collegiate," Marc Iavaroni said in the locker room before the rematch.

It was 22-4 Sixers, when Jack McMahon arrived at the Spectrum from the Palestra, where he had been scouting a college game. Fearing that he would jinx the team, he decided against sitting on the bench.

But there was little chance that anything was going to deter us that night. And as the onslaught continued, Moses Malone could not resist rubbing it in: "High-five now," he advised Wilkins. "High-five now."

CAUSE FOR ALARM

Years after the fact, Billy Cunningham would remember our 8-8 closing stretch as the "best thing that ever happened to us."

He didn't care about winning 70 games, something that was routinely discussed when we were 57-9.

"We only had one goal," he said, "and that was to win a title." So he rested guys, tried to get them healthy.

There was evidence that he was more concerned than he let on. When we lost to New Jersey on March 25, Billy told reporters that he was worried about the team falling into bad habits. When we fell in Chicago four days later, he said, "I don't like what we're doing. We're not running. We're not being aggressive. If it's not one thing, it's another. Our game is transition, and we're not doing that, either."

Then he decided that the team would practice every available day until the playoffs, something he reconsidered when we beat Atlanta the following night to clinch the best record in the East.

A bad shot by Andrew Toney late in an April 6 loss to San Antonio led Billy to drop-kick an ice bag over press row. A 19-point loss to Washington a week later—"by far the worst performance" of the year, he later told reporters—prompted him to call for practice an hour earlier than usual the next morning.

But here was the biggest concern of all: Moses Malone was hurting. He first complained of soreness in his right knee during an April 10 victory over the Knicks, a game in which he shot 2-for-7 from the field—season lows for field goals and attempts—and failed to grab an offensive board for the first time all year.

Diagnosed with tendonitis in that knee, he sat out the last four regular-season games. So while his 1,194 rebounds were the fourth-best total in team history—and 181 more than Darryl Dawkins and Caldwell Jones had grabbed between them in 1981-82—and while we became, at 65-17, the fifth team in NBA history to win 64 games or more, there was cause for alarm.

"Will Moses Be Able to Play?" the *Daily News* asked in a screaming front-page headline on April 21. Nobody knew for sure. Four days earlier, after a season-ending loss to Boston, Billy said that he thought Moses would be ready for the playoffs, but there was no way of knowing how effective he would be.

In our favor was the fact that he would have time to rest. We had a first-round bye, part of which we spent back at Franklin & Marshall College in Lancaster—the site of our preseason camp—for a minicamp. But no sooner had Moses arrived than he had to be hustled back to Dr. Michael Clancy's office in Fort Washington; he now had fluid on his left knee.

"We knew he was all right," Julius Erving recalled. "Besides, Moses at 70 percent was still better than most centers."

Which is easy to say now. At the time, said *Camden Courier-Post* reporter Don Benevento, "There was a lot of fear that he wasn't going to be able to play."

"That was the only nervous time we had all year," said our equipment manager, Jeff Millman, who drove Moses to Dr. Clancy's office in his Ford station wagon.

Clancy's prognosis? The right knee was good, the left knee fair.

"I'll play," Moses told reporters two days before we were to face New York, which had knocked off New Jersey in a first-round miniseries.

He had worked out in ten-minute intervals that day, and only in halfcourt drills, but he would not recall having any serious difficulties. All he needed to do was adorn each knee with a neoprene sleeve, turn, and go to the rack.

But before that, he had something to say. Something nobody would ever forget.

14

"Fo', fo', fo'" would be engraved on our championship rings, and embedded in everyone's memory.

It was our battle cry, though it was never intended to be one, and it is the subject of some debate now that memories have been dimmed by the passage of two and a half decades.

Did Moses Malone say it in the Spectrum trainer's room, as Billy Cunningham recalled? In the arena's locker room, as sportswriter Jack McCaffery remembered? After practice at St. Joe's, as a radio reporter named Don Henderson says? Or from the driver's seat of his GMC Jimmy, as John Kilbourne believes?

And is it not possible that this is some sort of urban legend—that he never really said it at all?

"Some doubt whether he did or he didn't," retired *Inquirer* columnist Bill Lyon said. "My vote is, if he didn't, he should have."

He did. Moses confirmed as much, and Henderson and McCaffery were among the group of reporters that heard him say it. So too was the *New York Times'* Roy S. Johnson.

But Henderson, who then worked for WCAU-AM, said it happened after practice at St. Joe's. "That's exactly when he said it," Henderson said. "We were all down in the locker room, just prior to going into postseason play."

McCaffery, then working for the *Trenton Times,* agrees that Malone said it right before the playoffs, but remembers it happening while Moses was seated in his spot in the Spectrum locker room—which, by the way, was right next to the trainer's room.

"My recollection is, it was some sort of pre-playoff media event," McCaffery said. "There were a lot of people in the room at the time. . . . My recollection is, he said it's going to be a long process. We have to win four, then another four, then four again."

But Kilbourne remembered Moses being trailed out to his vehicle by a group of reporters after practice at St. Joe's, and the *Inquirer's* George Shirk asking him how he thought the playoffs would go. Kilbourne said Moses, already behind the wheel of his Jimmy, rolled down the window, uttered "Fo', fo', fo'," rolled the window back up, and drove off.

Shirk did not recall that exchange.

Billy Cunningham is just as insistent that Moses said it to him, and only him, while seated in the trainer's room. And Phil Jasner recalls Billy's bemused expression immediately afterward, as he wondered just what his center might have meant—raising the possibility that Malone might have said it more than once.

The impact was widespread. The Lakers' Michael Cooper said he hated the fact that Moses made such a brash prediction. Others, like Milwaukee forward Paul Pressey, secretly admired it.

"Just like Muhammad Ali, Moses put it right out there in everyone's face," Pressey said, "and almost backed it up."

The intent was never to make a grand proclamation: "We had played so many games during the regular season, and I just felt, why play 21 more in the playoffs?" Moses recalled. "Just win 12 more and go home to rest up for the next year. I spoke to a group of writers, and I was serious. It was no joke, because I felt we could go fo', fo', fo' and have a big ending."

As Matty Guokas said, "It wasn't brash. It was just his way of saying, 'We won 60. If we do what we normally do, we should go right through it.'"

"He said it in a very matter-of-fact way—no big deal in his tone of voice or speaking style," Roy S. Johnson said. "Moses believed it and just laid it out there."

Which was typical of Malone. "Moses wasn't real cocky," said Bobby Jones. "He was telling you what he thought. Moses was never one to exaggerate or blow things out of proportion."

But once word got out about what he said, the phrase took on a life of its own.

"It turned into Babe Ruth pointing into the bleachers and hitting a home run there," Marc Iavaroni said.

OPENING SALVO

Before Game 1 of our series against the Knicks, New York center Marvin Webster took a peek at the basket where the 76ers were warming up. Then he smiled.

Moses Malone sure didn't look all that injured to him. Thirty-eight points and 17 rebounds confirmed as much.

"Y'all make it sound like I'm dyin' here," Moses told reporters after the 112-102 victory. "I told you, everything's going to be all right."

Billy Cunningham hadn't been so sure. All game long he had been in Al Domenico's ear, asking him if it looked like Moses was limited in any way, or if he might be growing fatigued. Billy later told reporters he was "very concerned."

"I didn't know what to expect," he said. "I was concerned about his stamina, how he would go to the boards, and a million different things."

Moses wound up with 125 points and 62 rebounds in the series, a four-game sweep. Webster and his backup, Bill Cartwright, combined for 60 and 36, respectively.

"I never saw a player dominate a series more than he dominated the Knicks series," Benevento said.

"He was the difference in the two teams," said Rory Sparrow, a Knicks guard that year.

But Moses would need some help.

RALLYING POINT

The Knicks led by 18 at halftime of Game 2, and Billy aired out the team in the locker room, using more colorful language than usual. He could do that, he later told reporters, for one simple reason: "Bobby wasn't there."

Bobby had the flu, and Andrew Toney sat out with a bruised thigh. And the deficit, despite Billy's oratory, grew to 20 a little over a minute into the third quarter.

But the Knicks only scored one point over the next nine minutes, 43 seconds. One point!

Maurice Cheeks simply wouldn't allow them to advance the ball upcourt, wouldn't allow them to get into their offense. Years later, Hubie Brown noted that "in that series they were more dangerous when we had the ball." And this was a case in point.

With Toney out, Cheeks also took on increased responsibility at the other end, scoring 26 points. Eighteen came in the second half, three on a one-on-two fast break where he dribbled between his legs, knifed between Paul Westphal and 7-foot Bill Cartwright, scored, and drew a foul.

The Sixers, within three after outscoring the Knicks 24-9 in the third, finally caught up in the final period, en route to a seven-point victory. Moses had 19 of his 30 points in the second half, and 10 of his 17 rebounds. He also shut down Truck Robinson defensively.

The New York writers pounced. Cartwright, a target all season, was once again skewered, after going scoreless for the first time in his four pro seasons.

"And 'Invisi-Bill' was at his 'Invisi-Bill' worst," a reporter, explaining a computer garble to his editor, yelled into a phone. "That's I-N-V-I-S-I . . . "

UNLIKELY HERO

Years before, Franklin Edwards and his buddies would hop a train in Harlem and head downtown to Madison Square Garden to watch their beloved Knicks. They didn't have enough money for a ticket, but that didn't matter. They had their friend Tony, who worked as a hot-dog vendor inside.

"Some nights," Frank said, "he would open up a side door for us, and about eight of us would sneak in."

They usually found a place to sit in the blue seats, in the Garden's upper reaches. Sometimes, if it were a blowout, they would sneak down closer to the court. And if they were feeling particularly brazen, they would run across it at night's end.

All of them surely dreamed of playing there one day. Only one of them did. Even so, it was surprising that Frank was on the court in the closing seconds of Game 3; he seldom played in crunch time. But with Andrew still hurting, he had emerged as the best alternative in a tie game.

But that didn't mean he expected to win the sucker.

"The thing I remember most about that situation was that as we walked out of the timeout huddle, I was thinking, 'I'm in Madison Square Garden and it's probably the last play of the game, and I'm the last guy in this city anybody thinks is going to take this shot,'" he recalled.

We had been up 105-99 with 50 seconds left, after Moses beat the shot clock with a jumper and then turned a Maurice Cheeks steal into a spinning, weaving, court-length, layup-producing slalom. The play would lead Earl Cureton to call Moses "Magic," and still had Hubie Brown shaking his head years after the fact. Hubie said it was "one of the best plays ever by a big man in a pressurized game."

But the Knicks came back to tie it, and on the ensuing possession, they double-teamed Julius Erving on the right side of the floor. He swung it to Frank, on the left of the key.

"The key to the play was that Julius gave me the ball," he said. "That showed me he had confidence in me."

And, he added, "I knew what I had to do once I got it. Once I got the ball, there was no question in my mind I would hit the shot."

His confidence had been buoyed in the next-to-last regular-season game, when he made a buzzer-beater to nip New Jersey. That shot, Doc had told reporters at the time, represented Frank's "official arrival."

"That shot prepared me for the next moment," Edwards said. "That's why, when I caught the ball, there was no fear. I had done it before. . . . As soon as it left my hand, I knew it was good."

The 14-foot banker dropped the Knicks into a 3-0 hole.

"I lost more friends from that shot," he said, laughing. "I went up to Harlem, and everybody told me how much money they lost on me."

CLOSING TIME

We won the four games against New York by a total of 22 points.

"No man likes to go out 0-4," Hubie told reporters at the time, "but it was no knockout."

We had achieved the desired result, though. "All the games were close," former *Inquirer* beat writer George Shirk remembered, "and the Knicks were never going to win."

FAMILIAR FACES

If our road to the NBA Finals usually went through Boston, there was often a stopover in Milwaukee along the way. We had faced the Bucks in the Eastern Conference semifinals in 1981 and '82, beating them in seven games the first of those seasons, six the second.

Now here they were again, this time in the Eastern Finals, and after sweeping Boston, no less—the culmination of what Kevin McHale, speaking years after the fact, called "an odd season" for the Celtics.

Brian Winters, a Bucks guard that year, recalled that Boston "seemed to be in a little disarray."

"Bill Fitch was their coach," he said, "and they didn't seem to like him."

Boston Globe columnist Dan Shaughnessy was much more blunt: "They'd stopped listening to Bill Fitch," he said. And indeed, Fitch would be replaced by K.C. Jones after the season.

The Bucks, as always, had some skilled perimeter players, like Sidney Moncrief, Junior Bridgeman, and Marques Johnson. But their attempts to fortify themselves in the post hadn't worked out as well as they might have liked. Bob Lanier, who came over from Detroit in a 1980 trade, was 34 and playing on aching knees. Dave Cowens, acquired before the '82-83 season from Boston for point guard Quinn Buckner, had had to shut it down after 40 games because of a knee problem of his own.

That year, as in most of those years, it seemed to Lanier that the Bucks were "a man short" against us. He knew he would have his hands full with Moses. And Winters, a shooting guard pressed into service at the point (and playing with a bad back that would force him to retire at season's end), was wary of Maurice Cheeks.

"He would always steal at least one ball from me, every game," Winters said. "I had it in my mind it was going to happen. As long as it was only one, I was happy."

Lanier could relate. It seemed as if Cheeks—or, as Lanier still called him years later, "that damn Maurice Cheeks"—was always sneaking up behind him and poking the ball free.

"What he would do is, he would come from your blind side—the baseline side—and create havoc," Lanier said. "You would never see him coming."

But the Bucks were undeterred: "We were sky high," Johnson said. "We were confident we could beat them."

"We felt if we could beat Philly in Game 1, we had an excellent chance to upset them," Bridgeman said. "We believed if we won the game, it would knock them back on their heels."

It didn't happen. Bobby Jones saw to that.

THE STEAL

The Bucks were up one in overtime. We were without Julius Erving and Andrew Toney, both of them having fouled out. Moses Malone was having a miserable time of it, missing nine of his 14 shots and committing nine turnovers. Just 1:35 remained. Alton Lister was trying to inbound under his own basket.

Bobby Jones darted in front of Marques Johnson, stealing Lister's pass. While teetering on the baseline, he turned and feathered a pass to Clint Richardson, who dunked as he was fouled.

The three-point play was the difference in a 111-109 victory.

"The steal was so great, but with his momentum, I was afraid Bobby might throw the ball too hard, or not in the right spot," Clint told reporters after the game. "But it was such a soft, easy pass, I would've done him an injustice if I hadn't scored. . . . I think I put half my hand through the rim."

Years later, Bobby still remembered the steal. But he remembered Clint's reaction to the steal even more vividly: "He loved that," Bobby said of his friend. "He would talk about that a lot."

Among other things, Clint scored all seven of our points in the extra period.

"I remember thinking, 'We've got one guy making $5 million and another making $5 million, and I scored all the points in overtime,'" he said. "It doesn't make any sense."

Nor, Winters remembered, did his last-second miss from three-point range, which would have allowed the Bucks to pull it out. "I thought I made it," he said. "I had a very good look. That shot was dead straight, but it was a touch long."

The series was just getting started. So was Bobby.

THE BLOCK (OR WAS IT?)

In Game 2 at the Spectrum, the Bucks were within two with just over two minutes left. Winters, starting on the left wing, took a pass from Lanier and went hard to the basket.

Bobby was waiting. He wasn't supposed to be. The Bucks had hoped his man, Marques Johnson, would draw him out of the paint. But as Marques later told reporters, "He wasn't a good boy. He didn't come."

But he was all over Winters

"I took it to the hole really hard, and got slammed to the floor—no call," Winters remembered. "That's the way it goes. In today's NBA I'd probably be shooting two free throws, and we'd get the ball on the side."

Instead, Julius Erving wound up with a dunk at the other end, and we were en route to an 87-81 victory.

"No contact?" *Milwaukee Journal-Sentinel* reporter Tom Enlund asked referee Earl Strom from his baseline seat during the timeout that followed.

"Did you hear a whistle?" Strom shot back.

"I probably fouled him," Bobby said, years later. "There was a lot of contact. But it was the playoffs. Things are not called as much. We were fortunate there."

There's no question about that in Lanier's mind: "He fouled the guy on the play," he said. "You get away with it maybe because of who you are."

Years later, Lanier and Jones appeared at a school on behalf of the NBA. "Don't I owe you something?" Lanier asked.

He doesn't remember Bobby's reply. But he does know that that play is one that "stays on your mind, probably forever."

"As soon as I saw him, the first thing I thought about was that block," Lanier said. "That changes the course of time. That put them where they needed to be."

THE REST OF THE FI'

We won the third game in Milwaukee, surging from behind down the stretch. And just as the luckless Winters might have expected (if not feared), Cheeks did strip him of the ball in the pivotal run, en route to a layup.

Lanier carried the Bucks to a victory in Game 4, the one and only time *Camden Courier-Post* beat writer Don Benevento sensed the Sixers eased off the throttle during the postseason.

Mark Whicker, then a *Philadelphia Daily News* columnist, doesn't remember it quite that way. He remembers the players being "very upset" by the loss, maybe even "shocked."

The bigger shock might have been provided by Julius after the game. "I'll be back," he told reporters. But he then left the arena without further comment, as did most of his teammates.

"That was the only time I saw Julius stiff the media," Benevento said.

"I wasn't happy with the strategy and matchups that day and how I was used," Doc recalled. "I was upset with the ending of the game and had nothing to say to anyone. I just went back to the hotel to think about the game."

The *Daily News'* Stan Hochman called it "a classless stampede" in his column, and wrote that "through the years the Sixers have had all the public relations savvy of a startled cobra. Nasty, unpredictable, venomous. Julius Erving kept bailing out the organization."

In Game 5 Doc bailed us out with 25 points. The Bucks were done.

"They're the next world championship team, in my opinion," Milwaukee coach Don Nelson told reporters. "They play a different style in the West, but I can't see any team touching them."

Fo' victories to go.

15

The winners write the history. And history says we swept the Lakers in the Finals, capping one of the finest seasons (and, to that point, the best postseason) in NBA history.

Only in the fine print is it noted that the Lakers were without James Worthy, their sensational rookie forward. He had broken a leg late in the regular season, leading them to sign none other than Steve Mix.

Moreover, Bob McAdoo, Los Angeles' top frontcourt sub, was laboring with a pulled thigh muscle. And starting guard Norm Nixon suffered a slight shoulder separation when he collided with Andrew Toney early in Game 1, rendering him ineffective the rest of the series.

"I'm sure L.A. was looking at it as, 'If only we had Worthy instead of Steve Mix, we could have won that thing,'" Mix laughed.

Some old Lakers do in fact look at it that way. Asked how the series would have gone if both teams had been at full strength, Kareem Abdul-Jabbar offered this prediction in early 2007: "Lakers in six."

His former teammate, Michael Cooper, did not disagree. "If we had everyone healthy, I don't think they would have beaten us," Cooper said. "But you've got to tip your hat to them. You play with what you have."

Others, like Steve Springer, believe it was simply our year. "That season was a culmination of all their frustration," said Springer, who then covered the Lakers for the *Orange County Register*.

"Maybe [the Sixers] don't sweep if those guys are healthy," said Don

Benevento of the *Camden Courier-Post*, "but I can't see them not winning that series."

"That team," Mix said, meaning his old one, "was just on a roll. It could have gone six or maybe seven, but I think the Sixers would have won."

Especially given the way Moses played. He outscored Abdul-Jabbar in the series, 103-94; outrebounded him, 72-30; and captured 27 offensive boards to Kareem's five. The Lakers tried defending Moses not with Kareem, but with blue-collar forwards Kurt Rambis and Mark Landsberger. Moses treated both with disdain.

"I don't understand why they got Rambis checking me," Moses told reporters after his 24-point, 12-rebound performance in Game 2. "He can't guard me. . . . They keep that little guy on me, I might have a field day."

He had four of them, as a matter of fact. But as in earlier series, others had their moments.

IT'S GOT TO BE THE SHOES

Clint Richardson, bothered for years by foot problems, donned a new pair of Nike high-tops at halftime of Game 1, after missing all three of his first-half shots.

"When I put on high-tops, it's serious business," he later told reporters.

He made seven of his nine shots after the break, as we came from behind to beat a Lakers team that was on a tight turnaround. They had closed out the San Antonio Spurs in the Western Conference Finals on a Friday night, and were then asked to come to the Spectrum to open the Finals on a Sunday afternoon.

Coach Pat Riley cried foul. He also said that if he had to devise a defense to stop Clint Richardson, the Lakers were surely in trouble.

"I'd rather be underrated than overrated," Clint told reporters. "If they want to underrate and underestimate me, that's their problem."

Richardson was reminded of Riley's words as he waited to take a bow before Maurice Cheeks' first game as Sixers coach on November 1, 2005. Normally an affable soul, Clint's face darkened.

"When I saw Pat three games later, he wasn't laughing then," he said, an edge to his voice. "He was crying."

THE HAPPY HOOKER

The Lakers grumbled anew when they went to the foul line just five times in Game 2, making three—both Finals lows.

Again we came back from a halftime deficit, as we would in all four games. But with 7:58 left and the Sixers leading by four, Moses drew his fifth foul. Clemon Johnson was unavailable because of a urinary-tract infection. That left Earl Cureton.

Earl had played six minutes in the playoffs over three games—all in garbage time, none against Kareem Abdul-Jabbar.

"In my situation I was always down on the totem pole," he said. "I always stayed focused. I knew it was my job to always be ready. I took every game as if I would be out there the whole game. Whenever Billy called me, I was always ready to go."

Abdul-Jabbar made four straight shots against Earl the Twirl. But with the Lakers overly Kareem-conscious, we managed to force some turnovers and push the lead to 11 in Moses' absence.

And Earl fashioned his own personal highlight. Isolated against Abdul-Jabbar on the right side of the lane with a little less than five minutes left, he fired up a Kareem-like skyhook. It somehow went in, Earl's only basket of the playoffs.

"It took a lot of courage to even attempt that shot," Billy Cunningham said.

"That [moment] will be with me for life," Earl said.

BIDDING FAREWELL

As Game 2 ended, the fans seated in Section E of the Spectrum—right behind the visitors' bench—rose to leave, and that's when it hit them: This was it. The Sixers were going to win the series, win the championship. And it was going to be a while before this group of fans, all season-ticket holders who'd grown close over time, would be together again.

They shook hands, wished each other well, and said they would see each other at the parade. And if not then, the following season.

Todd Shaner, a college sophomore, was part of the group. When we had our parade a week later, he instead chose to do some yard work and watched the event on TV.

"I said, 'I'll just go to the next parade,'" he remembered. "I'm not going

to kill myself to get down there, because I know there will be more. I'm still waiting for that opportunity."

PARTY TIME?

We won Game 3 in Los Angeles. The goal was in sight now, but Billy replaced it with another.

"We want L.A. in four," he told reporters. "We want people to remember this team."

He would retire to his hotel room to review tape soon after that, only to be interrupted by a knock at his door. It was Harold Katz.

"We're going to Vegas," Katz said. "Let's go."

Billy was in disbelief. No way was he going to celebrate before the job was finished, not given all that had happened, all that had gone wrong, in the past. He sent Harold on his way, and went back to his tape.

"As the coach, you can never prepare enough," he said.

Nor worry enough, apparently. Before Game 4, Al Domenico told Billy that Moses was having trouble breathing, having been caught in the throat by an Abdul-Jabbar elbow.

Billy went to see Moses, who was unconcerned. "Kareem doesn't want to see me anymore," Moses said.

CHAMPIONSHIP POINT

Twenty-nine seconds left. The shot clock melting away. Julius Erving matched up against a single defender, the ball in his hands, the championship—*his* championship—finally within reach.

The Sixers had rallied from a deficit that had been 16 points in the first half of Game 4, 14 at halftime, and 11 after three quarters. Doc had already done most of the heavy lifting down the stretch, stealing Abdul-Jabbar's pass and going the length of the court for a dunk, then converting a three-point play to put the Sixers ahead, at 109-107, with 59 seconds to play.

"It was almost the way you would write it in a movie," Benevento said.

"That was one of the joys of covering Doc," the *Daily News'* Phil Jasner

Julius Erving crashes into Magic Johnson in Game 2 of the Finals.
Philadelphia Daily News/George Reynolds

said. "He had an incredible ability to rise to the level and beyond what was necessary."

Jasner would later see it in guys like Michael Jordan and Kobe Bryant, not to mention guys he covered on an everyday basis, like Charles Barkley and Allen Iverson. But he saw it in Julius as much as anyone else.

"Don't ask them where it came from," Jasner said. "Don't ask them why. Nobody knows."

The lead stood at one point when Julius got the ball again, this time at the top of the circle. And standing before him was Magic, the guy who had tormented us in the 1980 Finals and again in 1982.

Now, however, he was just the first line of defense. Just another defender in danger of becoming a prop in Doc's personal highlight reel.

Erving jab-stepped. Magic tensed ever so slightly: much better to give Julius a jumper, rather than let him get to the rim. But Magic had given Doc just enough of an opening to launch from 17 feet.

The shot was true. Twenty-four seconds remained.

"When Julius made that jumper, you knew [it was over]," said Steve Solms, a longtime Sixers season-ticket holder.

Solms was seated in one of Neil Diamond's courtside seats, right next to the Sixers' bench. Solms' brother had made the arrangements.

Solms, a man who had made his fortune redeveloping historic buildings in Philadelphia (and elsewhere), had similar seats in the Spectrum. Years earlier, when Julius was introduced before his first game as a Sixer, it was Solms who ambled out to midcourt and presented him with a doctor's bag.

And now, closure.

"I didn't find that shot," Julius told reporters that night. "It found me."

THE DUNK

One of Harvey Pollack's exhaustive media guides lists Maurice Cheeks as having a stunning nine dunks during the 1982-83 regular season, four more in the playoffs.

Who knew? Who knew that he ever dunked before or after the night of May 31, 1983? And really, who cares?

"It looked as if he was running on air," the *Inquirer*'s Bill Livingston said, recalling the scene at the end of Game 4. "He dribbled the ball with his right hand and was slapping his side with his left hand. It was like he was riding a hobby horse."

Added *Daily News* columnist Ray Didinger, "That might have been the only time in his life he didn't hit the open man."

Reminded of the dunk in November 2005, Cheeks feigned exasperation.

"I should have passed that ball," he said, shaking his head. "I really should have passed that ball. Or just stood there and held the ball, instead of dunking the ball. I didn't intend on dunking that basketball. How many years ago was it? I did not intend on dunking the ball."

But he did, and in the process he created an everlasting freeze-frame.

"It was just the euphoria of it all," he said, "winning the game and realizing all those up 3-1s against Boston—twice. Them coming back and beating us the first time, and [us] winning the second time. There was so much."

Then he recalled that Michael Jordan made a video, "Come Fly With Me."

"I flew, man," he said, chuckling. "I didn't really fly that high, but for me that was flying."

And once again he swore that he did not see Erving running alongside him. "Even Doc said something to me on the bus coming back: 'Why didn't you give me the ball?' I said, 'Really, I didn't see you.' Then as I saw it again, I knew he was right. I would have given him that ball."

Few people were upset that he hadn't.

"It was the perfect way to end it," said Franklin Edwards.

"The whole thing was so un-Mo-like," Didinger said. "It was the perfect punctuation mark."

Even Julius could not be too upset, though he did admit that he'd "wanted to do something fancy." He said Maurice's dunk was "a joy to behold."

The only dissenting opinion is of the tongue-in-cheek variety. It comes from Jack McCaffery, then with the *Trenton Times*, now with the *Delaware County Daily Times*.

"That's what started the jinx," he said, referring to a major-championship drought by Philadelphia teams that had not ended as of April 2007. "Philadelphia hasn't won a darn thing since Maurice Cheeks didn't give it to Julius Erving to finish the whole thing. That story was supposed to end with Dr. J slamming the ball. That's my theory."

He was kidding. Probably.

16

By the end of the third quarter of Game 4, Jeff Millman had a decision to make. The Sixers were trailing the Lakers by 11 points, but the Sixers' equipment manager had ten cases of champagne ready for the postgame celebration—ready, but not on ice.

"If you ice it," the dealer had told him, "you own it."

Millman thought about it, and finally came to a decision: Ice it.

"I'm sure glad we won," he said years later. "I'd have had a hard time telling Harold he was getting a bill for ten unused cases of champagne."

They used every drop of it to wash away years of frustration during the chaotic, cathartic celebration that followed. The *Inquirer*'s Bill Livingston, unable to make it into the locker room because of a tight deadline, remembers walking by and looking in the door.

"All I saw," he said, "was a torrent of champagne going off."

Guys were flinging it, and guys were drinking it. Everyone except Bobby Jones. He gave his bottle to Julius Erving—after a long, meaningful embrace.

MIXING IN

Shortly after the celebration began, Steve Mix came by, still wearing his Lakers uniform. He claims that he and Erving, his former roommate, drank a toast. Doc says otherwise.

"I didn't drink champagne that night," he said. "I wanted to have all of my senses intact."

At any rate, Mix offered congratulations all around. A picture that appeared in the *Daily News* the next day seemed to show him pouring champagne on Earl Cureton's head, though he wouldn't admit to that, even two decades after the fact.

"I'm not sure whether I was pouring or not," Mix said. "I do remember going in immediately and congratulating everybody. I was happy for those guys." Steve also admitted to "mixed feelings."

"I wish I had had the opportunity," he said.

Erving also wished Mix had had the chance: "Steve Mix was my guy," he said. "I felt happiness in my heart after we swept the Lakers, but felt bad Steve wasn't part of the championship."

As Mix said, "You can't look back too much and worry about what happened in the past."

Lionel Hollins also joined in the celebration, having long before completed his season with the lowly Clippers. "I was pulling for those guys all year long," he said, "even though I wasn't there."

Unlike Mix, he didn't feel like he missed out on anything. "If I hadn't won a championship [with Portland in 1976-77], it might have been difficult," Hollins said. "But it wasn't difficult at all."

Larry O'Brien, in one of his last official acts as NBA commissioner, presented the trophy to Harold Katz. "The 76ers own this forever," O'Brien said.

League publicist Brian McIntyre was an interested onlooker. The year before, he had seen Billy Cunningham slumped in the corner of a restaurant in the Airport Marriott after we lost in the Finals to the Lakers. McIntyre said Billy looked "absolutely despondent."

Now Billy and Doc were embracing. McIntyre could feel the warmth, the sense of accomplishment.

"The exultation in the 76ers' locker room that night was one of the most unforgettable moments I've had in my NBA career," he said. "There was a unique sense of purpose to that team that you see very rarely."

The celebration was at full boil by that point. "The whole world was in there," Clint Richardson said. "Guys were in there that we didn't even know."

TOUCH OF CLASS

Steve Solms, the longtime season-ticket holder, came in the locker room to join the celebration and was promptly doused with champagne by Billy Cunningham.

A little later, Pat Riley waded through the crowd to congratulate the Sixers. On his way out he was stopped by a camera crew.

"I'm gonna celebrate my team tonight," Riley said, "and I'm gonna celebrate Billy Cunningham, Matty Guokas, Jack McMahon, Moses, Doc, Andrew, Maurice, all of 'em, because I think they deserve it."

FULL CIRCLE

Cureton introduced Moses to a friend as "Al Capone Malone." That's because, Earl said, "he steals games."

Moses, wearing a tie over his sopping-wet jersey, seemed to like that. "That's me," he said, "the gangster of basketball."

Later Cureton asked Andrew Toney, in a mock TV announcer's voice, what was going through his mind when the final buzzer sounded.

"Man, I was so happy," Toney said, "I didn't know I had feet."

Off in another corner, Clint Richardson was so overwhelmed, he broke down. Bobby Jones consoled him, as did Billy Cunningham.

It was lost on no one that there had been tears in this very same room a year earlier, for a very different reason.

BUT FOR DIFFERENT CIRCUMSTANCES...

Mitchell Anderson, having finished out the season with the Utah Jazz, watched the finale at his home in Chicago. While he rued the fact that he "missed on a championship," he was happy for his former teammates.

"We had gotten close—me, Earl, Maurice, Doc, and Toney," he said. "At the same time, I was sad for myself."

Russ Schoene wasn't feeling much better. He was back at Tennessee-Chattanooga, recovering from a late-season back injury.

"It was easy to watch the games," he said. "The toughest part was the locker-room celebration. I was so close to being able to take part in that. I ended up having to turn off the locker-room celebration after a few minutes. It was tough to see."

Still, he said, "I was happy for them. I was real happy for Doc and the rest of the guys who had gone their whole careers looking for a championship. I was happy for Moses; there was a ton of pressure on him to bring one.

"All the guys on the team were good guys. Obviously part of you is a little upset not to be part of it, but what are you going to do? That's business."

Darryl Dawkins doesn't remember where he was the night the Sixers won it. It was not Lovetron, as far as he can recall. It was probably his mom's house in Orlando.

"It wasn't for me to say, I'm mad they won it and I'm gone," he said. "I was happy for those guys, because I feel like if we'd stayed together that year we possibly could have won it, but there are no guarantees in this game. I was happy for them. I wasn't one of the guys hating them."

PARADE PREPARATIONS

While the Sixers celebrated, Jack Swope, the team's 28-year-old director of marketing, was back in Philadelphia, hammering out details for the parade with Mayor Wilson B. Goode and his staff. Aware that the Flyers and Phillies had been mobbed when they rode in cars down Broad Street in earlier parades, the decision was made for the Sixers to ride on flatbed trucks with Plexiglass on all sides.

The other concern was the parade's starting point: that the players would be able to mount the trucks without interference from the fans. The place that was chosen was a spot near the Philadelphia Museum of Art. From there the trucks would proceed down Broad to Veterans Stadium, where the day would conclude with a rally.

"At one meeting," Swope recalled, "Mayor Goode told me, 'Some people are upset we're spending city tax dollars on this parade. Don't say anything. I'll take care of that. This is about our community, and this is money well spent.'"

PICTURE THIS

John Gabriel, the Sixers' video productions coordinator, videotaped the clincher, then packed up his camera and fought through the Forum crowd to the visitors' locker room. The first sight he saw was that of a tall brunette pouring champagne on the head of Matt Guokas. The woman was a team employee named Dorothy Summers; she and Gabriel would marry five years

Some 2 million people lined the parade route to catch a glimpse of the newly crowned NBA champions. *Philadelphia Daily News/Pat Bernet*

later, and they would have three children together.

After the locker-room celebration wound down, Gabriel made his way to the team bus. He was careful not to sit in the wrong seat, knowing that players usually have their favorite spots. Then he heard a voice: "Sit down here next to me." It was Julius Erving.

"You've done good this year, young man," Doc told him.

"I've never forgotten how he reached out and included me on that historic night," Gabriel said. "That memory has stuck with me all these years."

FLYING HIGH

The team flew home on a flight that had originated in Hawaii. One of the passengers was an 80-year-old woman returning from vacation.

"These guys are huge," she said. "Who are they?"

Irv Block, a Sixers fan who had made the trip to L.A., turned in his seat and told her. He informed her they had just won a championship, too.

But she wasn't done. "How much do they make?" she asked.

Block told her what he knew.

"That's amazing," she said. "This is the first time I've been on a flight where the people are worth more than the airplane."

PASS THE TROPHY, PLEASE

A huge crowd awaited the team at the airport in Philadelphia. As the players filed off the plane, John Gabriel noticed that the championship trophy had been left behind. He mentioned it to Millman, saying that if they were to carry it off, they would be in "every newspaper in the world" the following day. But Billy Cunningham scuttled their plan.

"Gimme that thing," he said.

But he didn't get far, either.

"I remember his glasses went sideways, and we had to grab the trophy from him, because he almost dropped it," Clint Richardson said.

THE LAST DETAIL

Soon after the plane landed, Andrew Toney, Maurice Cheeks, and Earl Cureton made their way to the home Caldwell Jones maintained in Philadelphia.

C.J., who had happily watched the final game with some friends, met his old teammates out in his driveway. They hugged, and somebody broke out a bottle of champagne for one last toast.

"This makes it official," someone said.

JOYRIDE FOR SOME

The parade was held on June 2. As planned, the players met at the Museum of Art and boarded the flatbed trucks for the trip down Broad Street to Veterans Stadium.

"I'll never forget [it]," Matt Guokas said. "It was such a beautiful day, and the fans were drinking it all in."

Phil Jasner will never forget that day either. As soon as reporters boarded the truck set aside for them, it blew a tire.

"Didn't just blow a tire," he corrected. "But it came apart so that all that was there was an iron rim. The idea was to take notes, but you couldn't. . . . You couldn't do anything. You had to trust your memory. It was incredible. We walked around shaking after that, because it was the most ungodly ride you could imagine."

Jack McCaffery recalled the ride as "one of the great tortures I've ever had in my life."

They couldn't stop because the media truck was directly in front of the players' truck. So they continued on their bumpy way.

"I literally had to close my eyes," McCaffery said, "because I thought my eyeballs were going to come out of my skull. The flat occurred in the beginning. As we got closer to South Philadelphia, [the truck] sped up. I had my eyes closed and my hands on my eyes. The thing started to smoke. Bill Lyon's line was, 'Chariot of Fire.'"

TWENTY-ONE-PAIL SALUTE

Nearly two million people lined the parade route, making for one long, loud celebration. But certain moments stood out, as when the players' truck neared the Academy of Music on Locust Street.

There was some construction going on in the area, recalled Clayton Sheldon, then the Sixers' assistant director of group sales. About 30 workers were on their lunch hour, and seeing Moses Malone among the players, they raised their lunch pails in salute.

"That was a real tribute from a bunch of blue-collar guys to a blue-collar basketball player." Clayton said. "That's what Moses was—a grinder."

FINAL REMARKS

When the team reached Veterans Stadium, all the principals were asked to address the crowd gathered there.

"I know you're all season-ticket holders, right?" Harold Katz asked. "If not, you will be next year, right?"

He was booed.

"That was widely interpreted as a sales pitch," McCaffery recalled. "I don't think people were any too pleased by it."

Marc Iavaroni, caught by surprise when he was asked to offer a few words, said he only had two. Then he uttered four: "Thank you very much."

I read a poem I had written with a friend by the name of Ken Hussar, the self-appointed poet laureate of Salunga, Pennsylvania, in Lancaster County. It ended with this: ". . . and to our Sixer fans we say, 'Paid in full.'"

It was left to Julius Erving to tie a bow around everything.

"There was nothing pretty about what we did to the NBA this year," he said. "It was beautiful."

LOOKING AHEAD

Much earlier in the day, Ray Didinger had been driving to the parade, wondering what on earth he could possibly write about the team. Every angle had been exhausted; there was no new ground to be broken.

Then it dawned on him. He had seen a play by Jason Miller called "That Championship Season," about a high school basketball team's 20th reunion, a play that was later turned into a motion picture starring Robert Mitchum, Martin Sheen, and Stacy Keach. Didinger wondered, What would these Sixers be doing 20 years down the road?

Jack McMahon decided that Julius Erving would be president of the United States. And, McMahon added, Andrew Toney would be playing the Yul Brynner role in *The King and I.*

Bobby Jones would be a missionary, said John Kilbourne, the flexibility coach. Maurice Cheeks would be head of a baking company, said Al Domenico—"all chocolate-chip cookies."

And what of Moses Malone?

"In 20 years?" Mark McNamara said. "He'll still be leading the NBA in rebounding."

17

Micheal Ray Richardson stood over Marc Iavaroni, who was sprawled on the apron of the court in the Spectrum, and showered him with verbal abuse.

Richardson, the New Jersey Nets guard, had just streaked in for a layup even though Marc had tried to foul him—even though he'd tried to take his head off, really. And now he was letting Iavaroni know just what he thought about that.

The game, the fifth and deciding one in a 1984 first-round playoff series, was slipping away from us. We had led by seven points with seven minutes left, but now the Nets were making their move. Richardson's free throw tied it with five minutes to play, and New Jersey would close us out, ending our title defense almost before it began.

The Nets played free and easy throughout the series—an odd one that saw neither team win on its home court—while we played old and creaky. Darryl Dawkins gained a stalemate with Moses Malone, in the process exacting some measure of revenge against the team that had discarded him 20 months earlier. And other Nets, like Richardson, Buck Williams, Albert King, and Otis Birdsong, came up big.

Still, we had battled back to tie the series by winning two games in the Meadowlands, leading Julius Erving to guarantee victory in Game 5.

"You can mail in the stats," he'd said. But it wasn't to be.

Billy Cunningham said it ended "probably the way it should have."

"And," he added, "it told the story of our whole season. . . . Up seven in the fourth period, and you could just see that as much as they wanted it, as hard as they played, there was nothing in the tank. There was nothing there."

We won 52 games in the regular season, but only on occasion were we as dominant as the year before. While Moses again led the league in rebounding, his scoring average and shooting percentage sank; Billy thought he didn't get nearly as many calls as he had in '82-83.

There was some individual brilliance—Andrew Toney, for one, made his second straight All-Star team—but not the same collective effort, not the same drive. There were more injuries. Our defense wasn't as good. We didn't run as much.

"People just weren't together, or there wasn't the same energy level or attitude walking in the locker room or stepping on the court as we had the previous year," Billy said. "And rightfully so. They had achieved the world championship. It was just a different atmosphere. It wasn't the dream year we experienced the year before."

Clemon Johnson could tell things were different right away.

"When we got to camp in the fall of '83, we were still celebrating," he said. "A lot of us were not in top-notch shape and [were] carrying some extra pounds. We forgot we got that title with a lot of hard work."

Harold Katz agreed that the team was "a little complacent." When the season was over, Bobby Jones would be much more blunt: "Our attitude beat us," he told the *Philadelphia Daily News.*

The other problem was the approach of other teams. "We had targets on our backs as a result of the '83 NBA title," Johnson said.

"We knew everybody was going to be challenging us," Malone said. "We just didn't pick up the intensity like we should have done that first year [after the championship]."

One of the first challenges came, naturally, from the Celtics. During an exhibition game in Boston Garden, Moses scuffled with Cedric Maxwell. Then Larry Bird got into it with Iavaroni. And before anyone knew it, Red Auerbach came charging out of the stands and challenged Moses to take a swipe at him. (Asked about that instance after Auerbach's death in October 2006, Moses said, "Don't remember.")

Billy, who before the game had told Al Domenico that it was one of the few times he had been involved in a game in Boston Garden where he didn't care about the result, now found himself on the court, his sport coat ripped up the back, breaking up a fight.

The message had been delivered: Boston was back. The rivalry was alive and well. And the Sixers were not going to have the same cakewalk they had had the year before.

Although we won 21 of our first 26, we hit a lull. Billy tried pushing every button he could. After a road loss to Detroit, he convened a practice at St. Joe's solely devoted to rebounding, one that left everyone in a foul mood—especially Johnson, who stalked off the court after Maurice Cheeks, his close friend, accidentally poked him in the eye.

Harold chewed the team out in the Spectrum locker room after a February loss to a dreadful Chicago team, our second to the Bulls in four days. The next day at practice, Billy told his players that if he had to begin ripping them in the papers, he would. It was something he would never do; he preferred to deal with problems face to face. But it showed how desperate he had become.

"I felt my pleas to the players were falling on deaf ears," he said.

After Billy and Matty Guokas left the locker room that day, the players talked among themselves.

"As far as I'm concerned, two of the big reasons we're playing the way we're playing just walked out the door," one of them said.

Their motto became, "Just us," and that worked for a while; we won 17 of our final 23 games. But everything unraveled against the Nets.

"The physical wear and tear caught up with us," Erving said. "I had a strained groin muscle and could hardly run up and down the court, let alone chase Albert King all over."

He still believes we were a better team than New Jersey. But the Nets, he said, were "fresh, young, and hungry," while all the long playoff runs had taken their toll on the Sixers. And Billy does not disagree: "We had nothing left—nothing—and there was nothing I could do," he said. "I tried it all: yelling, cheering, etc. It was the most helpless feeling in the world."

The next draft brought Charles Barkley, and we returned to the Eastern Conference Finals in 1984-85, losing to Boston in five games. Billy retired shortly after that.

A year later, Bobby Jones retired and Moses Malone was traded. The year after that, Doc retired. Maurice Cheeks remained with the club until August 1989, when he was traded to San Antonio. That came six months after his friend Andrew Toney had retired at age 30, having battled foot problems for years.

Jack McMahon and I both left in June 1986. I went to Orlando, where the fledgling Magic was just getting off the ground, while Jack headed to Golden State to head up their player personnel department.

Matty Guokas, who succeeded Billy as head coach, was fired in February 1988.

The last link to the championship year—other than publicist Harvey Pollack, who's still with the club—was Harold Katz. He sold the team to Comcast Corp. in March 1996, near the end of an 18-64 season, the team's fifth straight sub-.500 campaign.

Buoyed by an energetic president (Pat Croce), a legendary coach (Larry Brown), and one of the great little men in NBA history (Allen Iverson), the Sixers rebounded, advancing to the Finals in 2001. But then Croce and Brown left (as did Iverson, eventually) and the team backslid again. The 2006-07 season, Maurice Cheeks' second as head coach, marked the third time in four years the Sixers had finished with a losing record.

Everybody else is a story unto himself.

DOC

Where was Cory Erving? For six agonizing weeks in the summer of 2000, Julius and his wife, Turquoise, waited and wondered.

Doc by then was working with me as an executive vice president of the Orlando Magic and living in nearby Alaqua Lakes. Cory, who at 19 was the youngest of the couple's four children, had had his battles with substance abuse, but his family was by that point hopeful he had turned a corner. Now the Ervings feared the worst. They made a public appeal in mid-June, two weeks after Cory went missing. He had been buying bread for a family cookout early in the afternoon of May 28 and had told his mom over the phone he would be home in 20 minutes.

He never showed up.

"It's a parent's worst nightmare," Julius told CNN's Larry King on June 23.

Doc told King the initial fear was "more along the lines of a relapse, maybe being on a binge." But as time went on, the Ervings worried that Cory had put himself in harm's way.

Rumors flew. Leads were investigated. Nothing panned out.

Finally, on July 6, a Volkswagen Passat was found in an eight-foot-deep retention pond less than a mile from the Ervings' home. Cory's body was inside. He'd been the victim of an apparent accident while taking a shortcut home.

"We are thankful to the Seminole County Sheriff's Office for bringing Cory back to us," Julius said in a statement. "We now have resolution. Getting closure was very important to the family in coping with this loss. We have learned a lot from this tragedy and we will be a stronger family as a result."

Instead, the family splintered. Turquoise filed for divorce in 2002, citing irreconcilable differences; there had been revelations in previous years that Julius had fathered two children out of wedlock, one of them being a professional tennis player named Alexandra Stevenson, the result of a tryst with a Philadelphia-area sportswriter.

"It tells you what is true about every player: That's how you know them—as players, as stars, as celebrities," Phil Jasner said. "Almost none of us have any idea what goes on [away from the court]."

When Jasner sees Julius now, he sees the same man he has always seen, feels the same warmth he has always felt. "I've tried not to judge," Phil said. "The decisions he has made in his life, that's his life."

It is the same with John Nash. "I've got problems in my own life," he said. "If I was as prominent as Julius Erving, they'd be all over the papers. Let he who is without sin cast the first stone."

Doc left the Magic in September '03 and in time settled in Utah. He continued as president of the Erving Group, a private investment company. He was named to the board of trustees at his alma mater, the University of Massachusetts. He commanded five-figure fees on the lecture circuit. Every now and then he did something basketball-related, as when ABC-TV trotted him out on a conference call in June 2005 to promote the network's coverage of the NBA Finals between San Antonio and Detroit.

A reporter asked Doc about his own experiences in the Finals.

"I was able to experience two ABA finals," he began, "the last of which . . . " He stopped, interrupted by chatter from an open phone line. "Go ahead, Dr. J," said a disembodied voice. The tone was curt, dismissive: *Oh my goodness, the guy's talking about the ABA.*

So Doc switched gears, and started discussing 1983, about what "an inspirational force" Moses Malone had been. About how great it was that four guys from that team made the All-Star team. All in all, Doc concluded, it was "a very, very successful NBA season."

Yeah, you might say that.

A VOICE STILLED

Doc had given the eulogy at the funeral of Dave Zinkoff after The Zink died at the age of 75 of heart failure on Christmas Day 1985.

"Of all the qualities that I can think of that he possessed, the most natural to him was not his voice or his mastery of a phrase," Julius told a crowd of mourners. "To me, it was his servicing of friendships. . . . Dave Zinkoff was my grandfather, father, brother, and son all rolled into one giving, sharing, loving person who cannot and will not be replaced. Ever. I long for the day when I can be a fraction of the friend that Zink was. . . . He was the best friend anyone could have. My friend. Your friend. We love you, Zink. Good-bye."

The Sixers had had a night for The Zink the previous January, at which point Erving presented him with a mink coat—a "Mink for the Zink," Doc called it—and the winner of a Zink sound-alike contest, Robert Freeman of Bensalem, got to call the third quarter.

While Freeman filled in, Zink went up to the radio booth to assist play-by-play man Neil Funk, in a manner of speaking. Though he was seated before a live microphone, The Zink insisted on calling out to acquaintances he saw in the stands. Cautioned by Funk about doing that, he protested: "But that was a personal friend of mine."

Hey, who wasn't?

LAST LAP

The Zink's successor, Jim Wise, began his first full season as the Sixers' public address announcer on October 31, 1986, when Indiana visited the Spectrum. He was eager to get off to a good start, and therefore mildly annoyed when Harvey Pollack handed him a folded-up piece of paper just as the game began.

"Read it during the first timeout," Pollack told him.

Wise said he would, but did not have a chance to review the note's contents beforehand. Another annoyance.

Julius Erving, left, and Moses Malone were greeted at the airport after Game 4 of the Finals by Julius' son Cory. *Philadelphia Daily News/Michael Mercanti*

When play was halted, Wise began reading the typewritten, three-paragraph announcement: "Julius Erving tonight announced that he is playing his final season in the National Basketball Association as a player." For a moment he thought someone was playing a practical joke on him. But it was true: Doc was done.

At every stop on his season-long farewell tour there were gifts: a putter in Portland; Napa Valley Wine in Golden State; a ski-resort vacation in Utah. And always he found the right words, the right way to say thank you. When they gave him a plaque in Seattle, he accepted it gratefully. And then, noting that it was November 11—Veterans Day—he asked everyone in the arena to pause for a moment of silence to honor the vets. In Sacramento they gave him a tennis-ball server. In Phoenix everyone was attired in surgical masks and caps. In New York they gave him two oversized aspirin, symbolic of the headaches he had caused the Knicks.

The pregame ceremony in New Jersey was the most moving of all. The Nets brought back several of his former teammates. They also invited his mom, and officially retired the No. 32 jersey he had worn while leading that team to a pair of ABA championships.

For once the Erving veneer cracked. He was moved to tears. "I'm not ashamed of that," he later told reporters.

STERN WORDS

The Sixers saluted him before his final home regular-season game, and there was a parade through Center City. But there were some discordant notes. When Turquoise sat down with Phil Jasner in February, before Julius' final All-Star Game appearance, she said she was "tired of the basketball life."

"Mostly," she told Jasner, "I'm tired of the people you have to deal with. My favorite time was when Fitz [Dixon] owned the Sixers. Everybody was close. There were no jealousies. I haven't enjoyed Harold. I didn't enjoy the New York Nets owner [Roy Boe]. But I loved every minute with Fitz."

Turquoise told Julius she would continue to go to the games, but no other team functions, including the Christmas party. "I've always believed you need a close-knit team to win," she told Jasner. "Boston has it. The Lakers have it. Here, I see jealousy. When I see selfish play, the enjoyment goes out of it. You can't forget about the people around you."

Some of her thoughts were reflected in Julius' remarks prior to his final home game, against Indiana on April 17. He said that when he returned in the future, he wanted to "know in my heart and physically see up in the rafters that this organization is a family." He later said he had asked Harvey Pollack about the history of the franchise, and wondered why there wasn't a deeper sense of tradition.

"I guess there were reasons," he told the crowd. "No player has announced before his last season that this was it. Everybody's been cut, traded, waived, or just disappeared. That's a poor testimony all around, and it smacked of instability."

LIVING THE NIGHTMARE

Erving had been the subject of a very public trade rumor (and also the subject of another very private, very brief discussion) before the 1984 draft. It was widely reported that we had discussed a deal that would have sent Doc to the Clippers for forward Terry Cummings. Less well known is the fact that Harold Katz proposed sending Erving to Chicago for the third overall pick in the draft—the pick that became Michael Jordan.

Katz initiated the discussion with Jonathan Kovler, then the Bulls owner, unbeknownst to anyone else in our organization.

Harold recalled, "I thought I had a deal. . . . [Chicago GM] Rod Thorn killed that one and took Michael Jordan. I would have made that deal." And taken Jordan himself.

Thorn said in April 2007 that the discussion never went very far. The Bulls were aware that Houston was going to use the first overall selection on Akeem (later Hakeem) Olajuwon, and that Portland was going to take Sam Bowie at No. 2. So the question Kovler posed to him, Thorn recalled, was whether he would be interested in trading Michael Jordan for Julius Erving.

Rod said he would not. End of discussion.

Harold said the Cummings trade fell through when Billy Cunningham quashed it. "And he was right," Katz added.

Publicly, at least, Julius did not say he was disappointed about the prospects of a trade. He did not have a no-trade clause in his contract, and he told reporters he appreciated the fact that Katz consulted him each step of the way. What Doc found more disappointing was all the leaks on the Clippers' end.

I said at the time that trading Julius would have been tantamount to trading the Liberty Bell or TastyKakes.

PUBLIC FLIRTATION

After the 1985-86 season, the Liberty Bell almost found itself on the shores of Great Salt Lake. Erving told reporters he felt like he was "being toyed with" by the Sixers in negotiations for his final contract, and Utah owner Larry Miller jumped at the opportunity to woo him out West, offering a two-year, $3.8 million contract.

I had gone to Orlando by then, but the Sixers thought they had reached a verbal agreement on a one-year, $1.465 million deal at the end of June, a deal that would have been finalized when the salary cap was raised on August 1. Instead, a three-week ordeal began in mid-July. It was one that saw Julius cut short a vacation in Jackson Hole, Wyoming, to visit with the Jazz. One that saw Doc's agent, Irwin Weiner, tell the *Daily News* that Harold Katz had "jerked Julius around for five months." And one that was ultimately resolved when Doc agreed to a one-year, $1.75 million contract after playing tennis at Harold's house.

"You [reporters] are so in awe of this man who came here and tried to take away a player who belongs here," Katz said at the news conference announcing the new deal. "I'm tired of hearing about Larry Miller. I'm not in love with Larry Miller. If I said he was my best friend, I would be the biggest liar in the world. I'm happy everybody thinks he was so sincere [about signing Erving]. I'm happy that I'm sincere and that Julius Erving is here. Larry Miller belongs in Utah and we belong here."

Doc spent some time as an NBA studio analyst for NBC, then came to the Magic in June of 1997, where he remained until September of 2003. A few years later he settled in Utah, nearly two decades after Larry Miller's very public flirtation.

18

The fan seated a row behind the Sixers' bench had some advice for Maurice Cheeks.

"Get 'em all moving, Mo," the man said in the second quarter of a February 2007 game against Dallas.

Cheeks couldn't quite hear him in the din of the Wachovia Center. "Ball movement?" he asked, turning toward the guy.

"Get 'em all moving," the fan said.

It didn't help on this particular night; the Mavericks, en route to 67 victories, won easily. And the Sixers, who long before then had jettisoned their two marquee players, Allen Iverson and Chris Webber, fell 19 games under .500 with a loss to Washington three days later.

But a funny thing happened on the way to oblivion: The Sixers started winning. They went 30-29 after Iverson was traded to Denver on December 19, 26-21 after Webber's contract was bought out on January 11. (He later signed with Detroit). And they finished a not-quite-as-horrible-as-expected 35-47.

"It was just fun," Cheeks said before the season's final home game, "putting guys out on the floor that were going out, night in and night out, and giving us a chance."

There was a 12-game losing streak early on. There was a 50-point loss to Houston late in the year. "But through it all I think our guys have become better people and better players from it, because they stayed with it," Cheeks said. "The fruits from all those things will come out later on."

Cheeks earned his share of the credit for keeping things upbeat and getting a young team to buy into his way of doing things, and also for encouraging his players to ignore the inside-out logic that being bad was good—that it would be better for the club to tank the season and enhance its draft position. (The folly of that was shown during the draft lottery in May. The teams with the two worst records, Memphis and Boston, wound up picking not first and second, but fourth and fifth, respectively.)

"[Cheeks] flat out said one day, 'Ping-pong balls take jobs. If you want to play for ping-pong balls, your job could be gone,'" guard/forward Kyle Korver said in March.

Instead, they were left with something far more valuable. They were left with hope.

WELCOME BACK

Cheeks, fired as the Portland coach late in the 2004-05 season, was named the Sixers' boss in May of 2005. Iverson, who knew him from his time as an assistant in Philadelphia, showed up at the introductory news conference and, sitting next to Cheeks, said he was so happy he wanted to "take him in the back and kiss him on his mouth."

The mood had changed dramatically by season's end. Iverson and Webber, said to be injured and unavailable, did not show up until minutes before the final home game—on Fan Appreciation Night, no less—and declined to sit on the bench during the game. Asked to explain their absence beforehand, Cheeks was at a loss, interrupting a meeting with reporters to confer with the team's chief publicist. When he returned, he explained that he had given the two players the night off, that Webber's back was bothering him and Iverson's ankle was sore.

Somebody asked if he had just reached that decision.

"In practice today, I didn't know whether or not they were going to play," he said. "I assumed that they were going to play, so I just made the decision that they're not going to play."

There was one final question: Was he disappointed that they were not there? Cheeks didn't respond, so the question was repeated.

"I'm done," he said, slumping in his chair.

The media pack then descended upon general manager Billy King, who launched into a profanity-laced tirade. But neither he nor Cheeks approached Webber or Iverson before or after the game.

Cheeks apologized for not being more forthright afterward, and the players expressed remorse a day later, before the season finale in Charlotte. At the draft lottery a month later, King announced that the franchise's goal now was "changing the culture," that everyone would be expected to conduct themselves a certain way.

It was generally assumed that either Iverson or Webber would be traded over the summer, but both were still on the roster when the 2006-07 season began. Cheeks had some changes in mind, though. He asked Iverson to let others, like forward Andre Iguodala, initiate the offense on occasion. And he cut Webber's playing time. Neither was happy. Before long, Iverson went to King and either asked the team to make changes (Iverson's version) or asked to be traded (everyone else's version).

The upshot was the deal with Denver, which brought point guard Andre Miller, veteran forward Joe Smith, and two first-round picks.

Before long Webber was gone, too.

Consider the culture changed.

BAD DEAL

Cheeks' 11-year tenure as a Sixers player came to an end when he was traded in August of 1989 to San Antonio in a deal that brought another point guard, Johnny Dawkins. That was devastating enough—Cheeks had always envisioned himself playing his entire career in Philadelphia, and had signed a one-year contract extension shortly before the trade—but it was made worse by the fact that Cheeks learned of his fate not from the team but from Michael Barkann, a television reporter for KYW, Philadelphia's NBC-TV affiliate.

At mid-day Cheeks was playing "Horse" with assistant coach Fred Carter in St. Joseph's University Fieldhouse. Coach Jim Lynam was also in the building, and he and Carter were well aware a deal was in the works.

"It was in the final moments," Lynam said in April 2007. "That's what [the front office] told me."

But Lynam didn't dare tell Cheeks, for fear that it might fall through. Instead he planned to break the news to him over lunch, once he was sure everything had been finalized.

The call came. It was done. Lynam went looking for Cheeks, only to learn he had slipped out of the building, destination unknown.

The Sixers were in a bind, since they had already scheduled a news conference for 2 p.m. KYW, thinking it would be in regard to a threatened move by Harold Katz to a new arena in Camden, New Jersey, dispatched a news reporter.

The reporter returned to the station and said it had nothing at all to do with the proposed move, that it was just something about the Sixers trading "some guy named Cheeks." Barkann caught wind of that, and minutes later he and his cameraman, Tom Foley, were out the door.

First they went to an apartment complex where they thought Cheeks lived, only to learn he had moved. Barkann, offering a bribe of two six-packs, learned from a maintenance man that Cheeks now made his home on Monroe Street.

Lynam had already been there for nearly two hours, waiting for Cheeks' return. "Then I reached a point where I incorrectly assumed, 'Yeah, I'll see him, but he obviously knows about it by now,'" Lynam said. "Well, he didn't."

So Lynam left moments before Barkann and Foley showed up. They rang Cheeks' doorbell, and not getting a response, wondered (like Lynam) if he had already been told of the trade and was holed up inside. Barkann called the station and asked what he should do. Stay, he was told.

Not long after, a black Mercedes pulled up, with Maurice Cheeks at the wheel. He asked Barkann and Foley why they were there, and Barkann had no choice but to break the news to Maurice.

"I need a minute," Cheeks said before driving off.

When he returned, he parked his car and said, "I still need a minute." He walked off and then returned to do the interview, teary-eyed.

"A Slap to Cheeks," blared the headline in the *Daily News* the next day. In the accompanying story, Cheeks said the trade "wasn't handled in a professional way," and added that if he had known a deal was in the works, he would not have signed a contract extension. "I feel betrayed," he said.

Lynam and Carter both expressed public regret, and Lynam met with Maurice late on the day of the trade. "It was obvious how bad he felt," Cheeks told the *Daily News*' Ray Didinger a few months later, before the Spurs were to play in Philadelphia.

Harold Katz also called the night of the deal, Cheeks told Didinger.

"He said it was a business decision; we had to do it," he said. "That was it. He never said he was sorry. He never said thanks for all you did. It was just like that, a business decision, cut and dried.

"After 11 years of playing—some nights on one leg or with one arm—that's what I got. I think I deserved better than that."

HOMECOMING

He was the first player introduced when San Antonio visited the Spectrum on November 16, and as the cheers welled up around him, he studied the floor, hoping they would stop.

They did not.

He finally waved, sheepishly. Maybe that would calm the crowd, get everyone to sit down.

It did not. A fan in the front row right unveiled a sign: "Maurice, There Is No Substitute." He wiped away a tear and finally—over a minute after it had started—the ovation died, not of its own accord but because public-address announcer Jim Wise felt compelled to continue the introductions.

Cheeks played his usual Cheeks-like game, with 15 points, seven assists, and a single turnover. Dawkins, who had inherited his spot, did even better—20 points, 11 assists, one turnover. The Sixers won.

Later, each agreed on one thing. "I'm glad it's over," Cheeks said.

"I'm glad he only comes once a year, just like Christmas," Dawkins said.

MORE MOVES

Cheeks was traded again in February of that year, this time to the Knicks. Two years later, he made a stop in Atlanta before winding up with the Nets in '92-93.

Late that season, he was standing at his locker-room cubicle, dressing after a home loss to Detroit. The smiling face of Pistons center Bill Laimbeer appeared around a corner.

"Man," he said to Maurice, "you was in the chamber tonight." The torture chamber.

Cheeks broke up: "Man, this guy . . ."

The 36-year-old Cheeks, by this point the oldest guard in the league, had entered the game in the second quarter, and it took the Pistons exactly eight seconds to post him up with Joe Dumars, who was two inches taller, 15 pounds heavier, and six years younger.

Dumars shrugged off a few bumps, turned, and dropped in a short jumper. Next time down, same thing: bump, turn, and score. Before long, Dumars had scored 10 straight points. And in the fourth quarter, Isiah Thomas burned Cheeks for seven in a row.

"They took turns tonight," Cheeks said.

He got the message, retiring at season's end.

THE ESSENCE OF MAURICE

He spent a year as an assistant in the CBA, then seven as an assistant with the Sixers. Next came three-plus seasons as the head man of an ill-conceived Portland team, a club with so many incorrigibles that it had long been known as the "Jail Blazers."

The highlight of his Blazers tenure had very little to do with basketball and everything to do with an old point guard handing out one more assist. Before a playoff game against Dallas in 2003, a 13-year-old named Natalie Gilbert was poised to sing the national anthem in the Rose Garden, Portland's home arena.

She started out well enough. Everything was fine through ". . . what so proudly we hailed." Then she faltered: "At the starlight . . . "? No, that wasn't right. What was the line? She just couldn't remember. So she stopped.

There were hoots from the stands as she held the microphone to her forehead, then turned to look for her parents in the crowd.

But before she knew it, Cheeks was at her side, saying, "C'mon, c'mon."

He put his left arm around her, coaxed her along. And if she stammered for a moment, she soon recovered her voice. By the time she reached "O'er the ramparts," she was again confident and sure.

Cheeks sang along off-key, encouraging everyone in the arena to join in. They soon did, their voices stirred by his act of charity. When it ended, Cheeks gave Natalie a hug and walked back to the bench. Cheers rained down.

"She just looked so alone out there," he later told reporters.

Gilbert would tell *ABC News* that if she was initially mortified, she came to regard it as "the greatest moment of [her] life." Billy Cunningham's mother was so moved by the gesture that she sent Cheeks a note. Hundreds followed suit.

Those who knew him best were not surprised.

"That's just so Maurice," said Laurie Telfair, his old friend from his West Texas State days. "That's the essence of him."

19

Andrew Toney might be "the greatest forgotten player in NBA history," as the *Boston Globe*'s Bob Ryan put it. But Maurice Cheeks never forgot his old friend and backcourt partner. Years after everything unraveled for Andrew—after foot injuries and an ugly feud with management short-circuited his once-promising career—somebody asked Cheeks about their collaboration.

"I dream of us," Maurice said.

The dream was still alive when Cheeks took over the Sixers. He wanted to hire Andrew as one of his assistant coaches. While the goal wasn't necessarily to bring closure to Toney's sad saga, that would have been the net effect.

Toney had seldom returned to Philadelphia in the years after he retired in 1988, at age 30, in the wake of accusations (largely from Harold Katz) that he wasn't as badly injured as he let on. And when Toney did come back, he never stayed for long. Now it appeared a new, happier chapter was about to be written.

But it wasn't to be. In a long e-mail to a reporter and in a rare (but brief) interview a month later, Toney claimed that he accepted the job two different times that summer. The Sixers had said that when they were ready to hire Toney, he couldn't make up his mind as to whether he wanted the job or not. By the time he said he would take it, they had decided to pursue other candidates.

"When Maurice talked to him, the job was there for him," general manager Billy King said in late September, after he and Cheeks met with reporters at a preseason luncheon. "I think Andrew was thinking about it.

It went back and forth. . . . It came to a point in time where Maurice said, 'All right, we're going to move on,' because I don't think he thought Andrew was ready to make the decision. And when he was ready to make the decision, we were at a point where we were moving on."

For his part, Cheeks said it was "just a situation that didn't get hammered out."

Toney claimed he first accepted the job via voicemail to Cheeks on June 26, the second time via fax to King on July 10. Ten days later, he was told the offer was off the table.

"The only thing Maurice told me—he didn't tell me why; he just told me they had a change of heart," said Toney, who emphasized he was "disappointed but not frustrated" at the turn of events.

"The only thing is if they could have been square with the public on the whole thing," he said.

He wrote in his e-mail, dated August 15, that he had grown weary of team officials saying they were uncertain if he really wanted the job, calling that "a press slogan."

Cheeks told the *Philadelphia Daily News* in mid-September that Toney was "not ready to make that step" and take the position. After the luncheon a week later Cheeks told a reporter that the whole hiring process was "a little drawn out." When asked if Toney actually accepted the job, he said, "I'm letting that go. That's a good friend of mine."

Toney had accompanied Cheeks to Chicago for the NBA predraft camp in early June and seemed poised to join the coaching staff.

Toney admitted in his e-mail that at one point in the month-long negotiations that followed, he asked the team to pay airfare for his family to fly in from their home in suburban Atlanta for some games. At another he asked the Sixers to buy him a house that could be sold after a year (with the team getting 60 percent of the profits, Toney 40 percent). At still another he asked them to pay for his lodging at an extended-stay hotel.

He emphasized that these were mere negotiating points on his part, not dealmakers or breakers. Whatever the case, the team declined to satisfy any of those conditions.

Later in the negotiations, he was told that the Sixers had 16 former coaches and assistant coaches on their payroll. He claimed that he responded by offering to work a year or two for expenses only. But he was denied on that front as well.

Neither King nor Cheeks commented on the specifics of the negotiations, which culminated in an offer of a one-year, $175,000 contract, Toney wrote.

But things went no further. "They said, 'We'll give him all the time he wants. We're just waiting on him.'" Toney said. " . . . They kept saying, 'We're waiting on his decision.'

"I was definitely looking forward to working with [Cheeks], but I'm not frustrated. I know how pro sports work. It just didn't work out."

So Toney remained an elementary-school health teacher outside Atlanta, where he lived with his wife, Priscilla. The youngest of the couple's three children, son Channing, was a sophomore guard at the University of Georgia that year, though he would elect to transfer to Alabama-Birmingham in 2006.

Andrew was in the Georgia Dome stands in September 2005 for a Monday night game between the Eagles and the Falcons. He wore the green replica No. 81 jersey of Eagles wide receiver Terrell Owens, another athlete whose stay in Philadelphia would end badly. The toned midsection of Toney's playing days was noticeably thicker; he had told a reporter two days earlier that he golfed, but couldn't do much more than that.

"If I go out jogging, I'll jog a lap and a half," he said. "Then it will turn into a limp."

Not many heads turned as he made his way to his seat in the lower stands, a few rows behind the Philadelphia bench; he was just some 47-year-old guy in a football jersey. But others knew better.

TRAGIC HERO

To former Sixers employee Tim Malloy, Toney is the "John F. Kennedy or the James Dean of Philadelphia sports."

"He's frozen in time," Malloy said, "and still carries the Boston Strangler image. No one sees him or can get to him, so he remains forever raining jumpshots on the Celtics' heads."

One such Celtic was Gerald Henderson, who said Toney would have been "a sure-fire Hall of Famer if his feet [had] held up."

"Any player of that era will tell you that," Henderson said.

"I still say he was one of the best two-guards to ever play in the league," said broadcaster Hubie Brown, the retred Hall of Fame coach. "Unless they played against Andrew Toney, people have no idea who the [heck] you're talking about."

That does not come as a surprise to Henry Bibby, now a Sixers assistant coach (and the player Toney displaced when he broke into the league in 1980). "As soon as you leave, you're quickly forgotten," Bibby said.

"That was one of Doc's things to me: Do as much as you can, while you can," said another ex-Sixer, Mitchell Anderson, "because when you're done, no one remembers you anyway."

Larry Bird remembers. Now the Indiana Pacers' president of basketball operations, he was sitting in the lower stands of a largely empty Wachovia Center two hours before the Sixers were to host Indiana in January 2007. Somebody mentioned Toney.

"You just never hear of that young man anymore," Bird said, "but he was so good, it was unbelievable. I really felt bad when he got hurt because he would have gone down in history as one of the greatest."

NEW SHERIFF IN TOWN

Twenty-seven days after we beat the Lakers in the Finals, the Celtics engineered a larcenous trade with Phoenix, sending backup center Rick Robey to the Suns for Dennis Johnson, one of the premier defensive guards of that era.

There was no secret as to why D.J. was in Boston: it was because of Andrew Toney.

The Celtics hoped D.J. would succeed where Henderson, Chris Ford, Danny Ainge, M.L. Carr, and Quinn Buckner had failed. He would finally put a stranglehold on the Boston Strangler.

Johnson knew that wasn't possible. He knew no one could really stop a guy like Toney, whom Johnson would one day rank just below Michael Jordan. But he could, he believed, curtail Toney's effectiveness to some degree.

"You can put a little more pressure on him, make him take shots out of character, or try to make him work a little harder," Johnson said in May 2006, nine months before his death, at age 52, of a heart attack. "I got up to play guys like that. I enjoyed the challenge of putting what I do best against what he does best.

"There are no losers in that. I'm doing what I do, the best I can. And he's doing what he does, the best he can. It's pure gamesmanship. I enjoyed playing guys like that."

While Toney still averaged 20 points a game in six regular-season meetings with Boston in 1983-84, his norm was down two points from the year before, five from the year before that. In '84-85, Andrew scored just 13.7 points against Boston in the regular season, 17.8 in five playoff games. By then his body had begun to betray him; he'd been slowed down by the only person capable of doing so—himself.

BATTLE OF BROKEN FEET

Andrew signed a seven-year, $4.7 million contract extension early in the 1984-85 season, which commenced the following year. He and rookie forward Charles Barkley represented the team's future, with Julius Erving, Moses Malone, and Bobby Jones nearing the end of the line.

But Toney was out of the game three years later, bitter and disillusioned after the Battle of Broken Feet, as it was labeled by the *Daily News'* Phil Jasner.

Andrew played in just 87 of a possible 246 regular-season games between '85-86 and '87-88. Along the way, he would tell the *Daily News* that he felt he was being treated "like a piece of meat—raw meat." He said management was a bunch of "jellyfish" and that he was getting "cross-eyed looks," always hearing "smart little remarks."

He told Jasner, "If a man is complaining about something as long as I was, someone should have been willing to research it. Don't say it's in my mind. Don't say the man doesn't want to play. I never laid down on any team. That's not me."

Asked about the situation in early 2007, Katz said, "Andrew had a navicular stress fracture, the same as Michael Jordan had in his second season. We all thought he could play, but Andrew felt he couldn't. We'll never know. The doctors I spoke with couldn't find anything [more]. It will always remain a mystery."

But at the time, it was just ugly. There were claims on the part of management that when Andrew was asked to do one thing, he would do the opposite. He was fined. He was suspended. He agreed to go to counseling, according to John Nash. He was asked to submit to a drug test, which he passed.

"The strain [on the respective parties] got to be so bad that there was a real credibility gap," Julius Erving said in a 1991 interview. "When it was deemed he couldn't come play and couldn't come back, he probably would have settled if he had been approached properly. But he just kind of felt, 'I'm getting told what I have to do, and I'm a man. I don't have to be told. I should be asked.' The proper means were not used to resolve the issue, so it became a Mexican standoff."

Erving, who was friendly with Katz and Toney, was loath to mediate the situation.

"That was their business," Doc said, "unless they invited me to come in and try to do something." He also believes both men might have been more willing to compromise if "so much dirty laundry hadn't been aired."

Toney did not show up for training camp in the fall of 1988, and the expectation was that he would retire. It became official the following February when he sent the team the necessary paperwork. He also issued a statement in which he said, "Retiring from basketball was not something I had expected nor wanted to do at the age of 30."

Matty Guokas, the head coach through much of the Battle of Broken Feet, thought the situation "needed to be massaged a little bit."

"[Toney] was not being believed, or he was pushed into something he wasn't capable of," Guokas said. "He didn't feel people believed him. He thought Katz was trying to push him through too much. Any player needs to be understood. They need empathy from the organization. The combination of the injury and the lack of empathy made the situation worse."

Nash could not even hazard a guess as to what might have resolved the matter, seeing as there was "suspicion on both sides."

"Andrew believed the organization betrayed him, and the organization believed Andrew betrayed them," he said. "If he didn't have a long-term contract, would he have played? I don't know the answer to that. Andrew was a difficult, difficult guy to understand."

And Katz might have been too direct for his own good. "Harold had an ability to convey the wrong impression. . . . He wasn't diplomatic in addressing his concerns," said Nash.

Postscript: The 76ers paid Toney $460,000 in 1991-92, four years after he had played his final game.

20

Steven Hunter, the Sixers' starting power forward in 2006-07, said one day late in the year that it was a "privilege" to be coached by Moses Malone.

It took Hunter a while to realize just how much of a privilege it was. "I had no idea he'd won three MVPs," he said.

Moses had returned as a part-time assistant under Maurice Cheeks in 2005-06, working with the big men, then became a full-timer the following year. That meant that Hunter and starting center Samuel Dalembert were constantly reminded about the necessity of turning and going to the rack.

Coincidence or not, Dalembert (8.9 rebounds per game) and Hunter (4.8) both put up career-high rebounding numbers, though it should be noted that Moses had an average superior to their combined norm (13.7) in seven of his 21 seasons.

TRADING DAY

"An old 31"—that's how Harold Katz described Moses on June 16, 1986. It was draft day, and it became a pivotal moment in Sixers history.

A trade of Joe Bryant to the Clippers seven years earlier had netted a first-round pick. Now that pick was the first one in the entire draft. But this was not a draft in which there was a clear-cut top choice. The feeling throughout the league was that North Carolina center Brad Daugherty was as good a selection as any, and we worked him out on the court at Harold Katz's home. He was a very sound player, as most Carolina guys are, and also very bright and personable.

Still, we weren't sold on him being the right guy for us.

"We liked him best," recalled John Nash, our assistant general manager at the time, "but it was more a case of, if we've got [Charles] Barkley and Moses, what are you going to do with Brad Daugherty? Even Charles and Moses used to fight for low-post position."

Then there was Maryland forward Len Bias. He was a spectacular athlete, but Jack McMahon had nagging concerns about him. And it wasn't drugs—Bias died of cocaine intoxication two nights after the draft, in which the Celtics had taken him second—but something Jack couldn't quite articulate.

"Even then we were doing background checks," Nash said. "We didn't find anything wrong with him." But we never bothered to interview Bias, never bothered to bring him in for a workout. In short, we were in a quandary.

Larry Bird, watching from afar, told reporters he was sure we would "screw it up."

In the meantime Moses' effectiveness was diminishing. His shot totals were going up, his shooting percentage down. His weaknesses as a passer and defender were being exposed. And some new concerns were cropping up.

On February 2 of that year, first-year coach Matt Guokas removed Malone with 1:12 left in a loss at Golden State, moments after a missed free throw by the Warriors' Larry Smith eluded Malone and squirted to Sleepy Floyd. As Moses stalked off the court, he began screaming at Guokas, and continued to do so as he plopped down at the end of the bench.

"Don't ever do that to me," he bellowed.

They met the next day after practice at St. Joseph's University.

"The incident is behind us," Guokas told reporters.

"I can't say that," Moses said.

A few months earlier, Malone's agent, Lee Fentress, had asked Harold Katz about the possibility of a contract extension even though Moses had two years left on the six-year deal he had signed with us in the summer of 1982.

"Harold was hurt by that," Nash recalled. "He was hurt by the fact that he wanted an extension."

But Malone had been just as hurt when Katz blasted him after a loss in

Julius Erving, adjusting some protective eyewear he wore for a brief period late in the championship season, played until 1987. *Philadelphia Daily News/George Reynolds*

Phoenix in March 1984.

"Is Moses Malone worth $2 million this year?" Katz asked a *Philadelphia Inquirer* reporter. "No. The answer is absolutely no."

"That ended up being huge—big block letters on the front of the paper," said John Kilbourne, our strength and conditioning coach at the time. "I remember at the time [Moses] said he wouldn't talk to Harold again. There was not much conversation between the two."

Katz had little interest in reworking Malone's contract after the '85-86 season. And everyone's view of the franchise's one-time savior changed dramatically on March 28. Struck in the face when Milwaukee's Randy Breuer swiped at a loose ball, Moses suffered a fractured orbital bone near his right eye, ending his season.

The Sixers, displaying a streamlined, fast-paced offense headlined by second-year forward Charles Barkley, won six of their last seven regular-season games in Malone's absence, beat Washington in a first-round playoff series, and extended Milwaukee to seven games in the Eastern semifinals.

They might have won that, too, if Julius Erving had been able to knock down a short jumper in the final seconds of the decisive game.

If it once seemed the team could not survive without Moses, it now seemed possible, even likely.

"MOSES IS GOING TO BE READY"

Moses further rankled management by not attending the Sixers' playoff games that year, choosing instead to go to the ones in Houston, his adopted hometown. When the Rockets hosted the Celtics in Game 4 of the Finals, CBS-TV's Brent Musburger asked him about the possibility of a trade.

"If he thinks the team is playing better without me," Moses said of Katz, "hey, it's up to him. But I know one thing: when I come to play, I'm coming to play."

Later, he added, "I would like to know before the draft. If Harold wants to trade me, I want to know [by] then, so I can get everything situated. . . . [But] please don't trade me to the East. I'd like to come back to Texas—Dallas or San Antonio. Don't trade me to the East Coast, 'cause Moses is going to be ready."

Before that, there hadn't been any discussion of trading Moses. But now the calls came. From Detroit, which offered Bill Laimbeer, Kelly Tripucka, Vinnie Johnson, and their first-round pick, 11th overall. And from Washington, which offered center Jeff Ruland and forward Dan Roundfield for Moses, along with rookie forward Terry Catledge and two first-round picks.

We wanted Cliff Robinson instead of Roundfield. The Bullets eventually agreed, and we settled back to consider our options.

SURPRISE CALL

In the meantime, Cleveland scout Eddie Gregory called, offering forward Roy Hinson for the No. 1 pick. That came as a bit of a surprise, since the Cavaliers did not have a general manager at the time—Wayne Embry had only tentatively accepted the position—and Hinson was considered a player on the rise.

So we met in a conference room in our offices in Veterans Stadium—

Harold, me, Jack, John, Matty, and assistant coach Jim Lynam.

It quickly became apparent that there was little interest in the Detroit deal. But Guokas, for one, was in favor of the Cleveland-Washington plan. He liked the idea of having taller forwards like Hinson and Robinson, both 6-foot-9, to defend Boston's Kevin McHale and Larry Bird. Nash liked Ruland's toughness. And the feeling was that Moses' time in Philadelphia had come and gone, that the best way to get back into the championship mix, to reverse the slippage that had occurred since 1982-83, was to make Barkley the focal point.

We decided to take a vote. But first Harold left the room.

"He went [elsewhere] and sequestered himself," Lynam recalled. "He said he was going to take a nap. He didn't take a nap."

Everyone gave the deals a thumbs-up. There was no dissent, though there was some lingering doubt.

"Nobody was real comfortable," Lynam said, "but as the conversation wound its way, it took on its own [idea of], 'Well, you've got to do what you've got to do.' This is not about sentiment. I think [it was] a little bit like going to the dentist—that's what pops into my mind right now."

Katz returned and signed off on it. There's no question that if he had wanted to, he could have vetoed everything right then and there.

And Lynam said, "I guarantee you, he gave thought to that. . . . If it was difficult for us, you can up it six notches for him."

There were other snags. We tried to get Cleveland to toss in its first-round pick, No. 7 overall. The Cavaliers balked. We countered by asking for cash—$1 million—along with Hinson.

That request, made via telephone, was my last official act as Sixers general manager. And when the Cavs countered by offering $800,000, I accepted, then went to tell Harold.

"Why didn't you get a million?" he asked.

Everything looked good on paper: Ruland, a rugged center, in the middle; two athletic forwards, Robinson and Hinson, to complement Barkley. None of the newcomers were older than 28. No longer would Moses be there to dominate the ball, slow things down, and get in Charles' way in the low post.

The face of the team had changed forever. The fortunes, too.

STOP THE PRESSES

"It's Matty's Team Now," proclaimed the *Daily News* the next day. Guokas patiently explained during a news conference that while he had had input into the decisions, he had not been the driving force; Harold Katz was the owner, and he always had the final say-so.

"It was going to be Harold's decision," he recalled in March 2007. "There could have been 15 guys in that room. A decision of that magnitude was going to be Harold Katz's."

Harold, in a first-person story that appeared in the July 1996 issue of a magazine called *The Fan*, wrote the following: "I can assure you that those moves were not my idea. We had a meeting and at least six of our basketball people were in favor of it, including Jack McMahon, who we had relied on for so long and who had been a brilliant personnel man."

Guokas said that before the deal was completed, doctors expressed some concern about Ruland's left knee, on which an arthroscopic procedure had been performed in March. Because of that, Guokas recalled, he and Lynam told the rest of the braintrust they were opposed to the trade.

But Nash does not remember the doctors having any deep-seated worries about Ruland's health. Neither does Lynam. "I think the medical consensus was that he was healthy," Lynam said in April 2007.

Ruland said he underwent a stress test on his knee after the '85-86 season. "And I blew it out of the water," he said in March 2007. "My left knee was actually stronger than my right. As far as anybody knew, I was good to go. No one knew [the extent of the problem]. I didn't even know it was as bad as it was."

"We all thought he could play through it," Katz said. "That's what our reports indicated."

So Harold, as he later wrote in *The Fan*, "ultimately approved the deals." But as he also wrote, "That was my mistake," although he emphasized that his "basketball people" advised him that it was high time to revamp the roster.

Ruland passed the physical we gave him after the trade, and on the first day of training camp that fall, he did well in the team's annual mile run.

"Almost beat Doc," he recalled, "at 275 [pounds]."

But Ruland realized very early that something was wrong; the knee just didn't feel right. He nonetheless played some exhibitions, one of them on a Tartan surface at the University of Alabama.

"That didn't help," he said.

"The next day," Guokas said, "he was hurting, big time. That was it for him, pretty much."

Ruland played the first two games of the season, then was examined by doctors who expressed surprise at the extent of the damage. He underwent an arthroscopic procedure, shut it down until February, returned to play three more games, then had to sit out the rest of the season.

Afterward, he retired. There was little choice. "It got to the point where it was bone-on-bone," he said.

Lynam understands now what no one seemed to realize then: that Ruland's legs "weren't made to support that [thick torso], especially playing this sport."

Ruland became one of the first people to undergo microfracture surgery—maybe the first, he said—and attempted a comeback with the Sixers in 1991-92. But that ended after 13 games, when a luggage cart pushed by a Celtics ball boy rammed into Ruland from behind as he waited to board the team bus after a game in Boston Garden on January 19, 1992.

Ruland, who suffered a torn right Achilles tendon as a result of the incident, later sued the Celtics but lost. He returned to play 11 games for Detroit the following season, then retired for good.

When contacted in March 2007, shortly before he was fired as the coach at Iona College, the 49-year-old Ruland said he needed a knee replacement and two shoulder replacements. "Some days are better than others," he said.

He's quite sure that if he had stayed healthy, the Sixers would have won a championship, and he would have made the Hall of Fame. "Coulda, woulda, shoulda—it's like being the world's tallest midget," he said.

The others acquired that day had knee problems of their own. Hinson, traded to New Jersey in January 1988, saw his career end three years later. Robinson played 131 of a possible 246 games over three years before he was finished, save a nine-game cameo with the Lakers in '91-92.

AFTERSHOCKS

The 1986 draft ultimately came to be known as The Drug Draft. Besides Bias, Chris Washburn and Roy Tarpley—the Nos. 3 and 7 picks—saw their careers cut short by substance-abuse issues.

Brad Daugherty, on whom the Cavaliers spent the first overall pick, averaged 19 points and 9.5 rebounds over eight seasons for Cleveland, but was forced to retire at age 30 because of persistent back problems.

Laimbeer and Vinnie Johnson made huge contributions to Detroit's championship teams in 1988-89 and '89-90, which were coached by former Sixers assistant Chuck Daly. So did the player the Pistons took at No. 11 in 1986, Georgia Tech center-forward John Salley. Kelly Tripucka was later traded for Adrian Dantley, who was in turn traded for Mark Aguirre.

LIMITED IMPACT

Moses Malone, who during his introductory news conference in Washington referred to Harold Katz as a "psycho" and vowed to "shut him up I-95" (the major highway linking the two cities) was unable to lift the Bullets out of the middle of the pack. They went 42-40 and 39-43 in his two years there.

He nonetheless continued to fire salvos at Harold.

"I've been over the trade," Malone told reporters in training camp. "I just didn't like the way he traded me. He traded me when I was hurt, so I'll never be at peace with Harold Katz because I know what type of guy he is."

His tone softened two days before he faced his former team for the first time, on Christmas Day in the Spectrum.

"I've got nothing against Harold Katz," he told a group of Philadelphia-area reporters after a Bullets practice in Bowie, Maryland. "He gave me a six-year contract. He's a great guy. I didn't like the way he [traded] me without giving me the chance to show I could still play, but that's a part of the business."

"Will you talk to him?" someone asked.

"If I see him," Moses said. "Maybe Harold will be the Sixers' 12th man. Tell him to come on down to the hoop. I'll meet him there."

Moses was accorded a standing ovation before that game, and then collected 28 points and 21 rebounds in a 102-97 Washington victory over the conspicuously Ruland-less Sixers.

"They need a big man inside," Moses told reporters.

When the two teams met again on January 10, Moses piled up 39 points and 17 boards in another Bullets victory.

After two years in Washington, he spent three in Atlanta and two in Milwaukee before making a return trip to Philadelphia.

LAST ROUNDUP

Moses landed back in Philly in 1993-94, having signed, at age 38, a one-year contract to serve as a backup and mentor to rookie center Shawn Bradley. Maybe he could play a little power forward, too.

"I've got a little power in me," Moses said during a congenial welcome-back news conference in August.

Early in the season, the Sixers were hosting Miami when Heat backup center Matt Geiger tried to deny Moses position in the post. Moses acted as if he had been bludgeoned by a crowbar.

Whistle. Foul on Geiger.

Moments later, the Sixers' Johnny Dawkins attempted a three-point shot. Moses, inflicting far more damage on Geiger than vice versa, established position underneath. Geiger pushed back.

Another whistle. Another foul on Geiger.

Geiger bounced the ball on the floor once, then again—harder.

The Heat's starting center, Rony Seikaly, was similarly bemused when he was called for two over-the-back fouls against Moses later in that game; after the second he tossed the ball high into the air.

Yes, the old guy still had some power. But only some. He averaged 5.3 points and 4.1 rebounds that year, then played 17 games for San Antonio in 1994-95, his 21st and final season.

He was elected to the Basketball Hall of Fame in 2001.

ONE MORE HOMECOMING

When Moses returned to Philadelphia for Maurice's first game as a head coach in November 2005, he was asked, predictably, about Harold Katz.

"A lot of guys think Harold was a bad guy," he said. "Harold was a great guy. Harold was probably the only owner I could talk to." He laughed.

Then someone reminded him that he hadn't been all that happy with his former owner when he had been traded.

"I was disappointed," he said. "When you're playing for the 76ers and you've got [allegiances] here, this is what you want to be—a 76er. You don't want to be traded to a team like the Washington Bullets. But I had to go where they wanted me to go."

21

The man approached Bobby Jones the night of an open house at Charlotte Christian School in the fall of 2002, his two daughters in tow. He told Bobby, by then a fixture at the school for over a decade, that he too had played in the NBA.

Bobby was polite, but skeptical. First chance he got, he went looking for a copy of the *NBA Encyclopedia.*

"He didn't really fit the mold of what I remember NBA players being," Bobby said. "He looked a little thicker. He looked more like a linebacker than a basketball player."

He discovered that the man—Bart Kofoed—was telling the truth. Kofoed had broken into the league in 1987, a little over a year after Bobby retired, and played five seasons.

Kofoed certainly remembered Bobby. He had been one of his favorite players while he was growing up in Omaha, Nebraska. And he remembered the 1982-83 Sixers. He was a high school senior that year, a budding player and a certified basketball junkie. He and his friends would get together to watch the playoff games. Over 20 years later, Kofoed said that the memory of Maurice Cheeks' dunk "sticks in [his] head more than anything else, by far."

Bobby, who spent 12 of his 16 years at Charlotte Christian as the boys' head basketball coach (doubling up as the athletic director for five of those years), was by that point an assistant to Shonn Brown. He asked Kofoed if he was interested in joining him on the bench, as a volunteer assistant. After filling that position for a year, Kofoed had a proposition for Bobby: Would he be interested in becoming a part of Kofoed's fledgling ministry, 2xsalt?

Jones conferred with his wife, Tess, and said he would make the jump, that he would leave a school where as head coach or co-coach (with Brown) he had won three state titles and coached a future NBA player (Todd Fuller).

"The timing was right," Bobby said. The youngest of the couple's three children, Meredith, had just graduated from Charlotte Christian, having followed older brothers Eric and Matt through the school. Bobby decided it was time for a new challenge.

He finished out the 2003-04 year and joined an organization dedicated to reaching out to kids in inner-city Charlotte. David Thompson, his former teammate with the Denver Nuggets, also agreed to come aboard.

"We started to use the platform of sports, mentoring, and education to reach these kids," Kofoed said. "Through that platform, we could share our faith. . . . It's not a conversion-by-concussion ministry. We're not there to beat them over the head with the Bible. We just say, 'Here's a game we loved and played at a high level. Look what it can teach you. We're going to tell you what works for us. It's between you and the Holy Spirit what you want to do.'"

The former players form a "three-headed monster," Kofoed said. He runs the day-to-day operation of 2xsalt, which during the school year mentors 50 kids in grades K-8 each day. Jones and Thompson organize the staff, as well as the ministry's many leagues, camps, and outreaches.

They wear other hats, too. When Bobby was reached by telephone one day in November 2006, he said he had been making calls, trying to find a crane. 2xsalt had bought the basketball floor the Charlotte Hornets had used in the old Coliseum, and now the organization had to figure out how to move it.

"Every week it's something different," Bobby said.

But the biggest part of the job is fundraising. And that, Bobby said, is "something I'm still not comfortable with."

He's fine with every other aspect of the move, though. "It's a path I followed," he said, "and we're going to continue to follow, not knowing what doors are going to open."

BEST SUPPORTING ACTOR

Bobby closed the door on his NBA career at the end of the 1985-86 season. That was not unexpected, seeing as he was in the final year of a contract. But he never made a formal announcement of his intentions. He had no use for such things. What he said, if asked, was that he and Tess had talked about it, and while they had not made a definite decision, he didn't foresee playing beyond '85-86.

Even in his last season, the White Shadow was asked to come to the rescue. The Sixers were 12-12 and showing their age, and no acceptable replacement had been found at shooting guard for Andrew Toney, who was bothered by his foot problems. So Matty Guokas rolled the dice, moving Julius Erving to Toney's spot and making Bobby the starting small forward.

The Sixers finished with a 54-28 record, even though Moses Malone missed the last seven games with his eye injury. Then they squeezed past Washington in the first round of the playoffs and extended Milwaukee to seven games in the Eastern semis.

Bobby told reporters it was "one of [his] most enjoyable times." The team, with Charles Barkley as its irrepressible centerpiece, played recklessly and unselfishly. And that was Bobby's preferred approach.

The fans had been letting him know for weeks that they would miss him once he was gone. They would walk him to his car after games and wish him well. They would wave to him when he stopped at a traffic signal. Bobby had not expected such an outpouring of affection—not from a city that prided itself on its toughness—and he was genuinely touched.

But his career had run its course. His kids were growing up. Too much of life was passing Bobby by.

It was left to *Daily News* columnist Mark Whicker—who had covered Bobby as far back as high school while working at a paper in Chapel Hill, North Carolina—to write the epitaph of Jones' career. He did so marvelously in a column that appeared the day after Jones' final game, the Game Seven loss in Milwaukee. It was entitled "The Best Supporting Actor."

Bobby told Whicker the game had been "fun," and that he was happy for Bucks coach Don Nelson and his team because they played the game "the way it ought to be played." He also said he was glad to be leaving the day-to-day grind of the NBA behind.

The interview over, Bobby approached the soft-drink tray in the visitors' locker room of the MECCA and grabbed a single Cherry Coke. Whicker found that significant. He had seen a great many other players—products of the grab-all-you-can era of athletics—shovel sodas into their travel bags and skulk out. Bobby Jones took one. Then he left.

"I'll miss that guy," Jack McMahon told Whicker.

"I'll give you a lot of help on that one, Jack," Whicker wrote.

CLINT

The day the Sixers were honored at the White House, Clint Richardson talked about his contract over lunch in the Congressional Commissary—how he was underpaid, how he wanted a new deal.

That remained his stance even though he continued to perform well in the two seasons that followed the title run.

He considered holding out in the fall of 1985—despite the fact that three years remained on his deal—then relented. In the meantime, we explored a trade with Indiana, one that appeared to have gone through the first day of training camp. There were still details to iron out, though. For the time being, Clint remained a 76er, albeit an unhappy one.

Standing in the middle of the gym at Franklin & Marshall College, talking to a single reporter, he could not hide his exasperation.

"What a mess," Clint said. "I feel a little let down because I've been fairly loyal to this organization, and I don't deserve to be treated like this."

The reporter wondered how much loyalty was worth. Richardson made a "zero" with his thumb and index finger. Less than a month later, amid the exhibition season, we sent him to the Pacers for two second-round picks.

Asked two decades after the fact if it was true he wanted a better contract at that point in his career, Clint said, "At first I did." But then Harold Katz explained to him that the team had just done a new deal with Andrew Toney.

"I said, 'Fine, if that's what it's like, let me finish my career here,'" Clint recalled. "The trade came out of the blue. . . . I was really disappointed when I got traded. I wanted to finish my career in Philadelphia because I'd promised my family I would play 10 years."

He spent two years in Indiana (meaning he played eight seasons in all), and has since returned to his native Seattle. He is now the coordinator of an elementary-school program there, and has talked of going into the ministry.

A regular at Sixers reunions, he remembers the victory parade as "an expression of all that pent-up frustration."

"That team never will be forgotten," he said.

22

Jack McMahon hovered in the back of the hotel ballroom that day in May of 1985, away from the cameras, away from the lights.

The focal point of all the attention was Billy Cunningham. He sat at the front of the room, in front of an overflow crowd of reporters, and said he was stepping down as the coach of the 76ers.

But it was not, he said, a day for tears. "I leave here with a smile on my face," he said.

McMahon was celebrating privately, quietly. Celebrating the coaching career of a man with whom he had worked for eight years. A man who in the beginning he had mentored, and a man who had come to be a friend.

"We've seen movie stars who start out [and you say], 'What a terrible actor,'" McMahon said. "You see them ten years later, and they're like Academy Award performers."

Which is the way it had gone with Billy. He left with a 454-196 record. He was a guy who'd grown into the job.

"It's like anything," McMahon said that day. "If you work at your craft, no matter what it is, and you consider it a profession and you treat everybody like professionals, it just comes to you. It becomes second nature."

Billy had been reluctant to get into coaching in 1977. He never thought he would stay as long as he did. He actually considered quitting after the title run, but signed a contract extension instead.

Now he was done for good, after a season in which we won 58 games and reached the Eastern Conference Finals, losing to Boston. He had been 90 percent sure of his intentions at midseason, but did not tell anyone in case he had a change of heart.

He didn't. And though he was not quite 42 years old when he stepped down, he never returned to the sideline.

He did have "one twinge," he told *Inquirer* columnist Bill Lyon in February 1986: "That was just before training camp opened [in the fall of 1985]," Billy said. "It lasted about 15 minutes. Then I found out that fall is a season. Now it's my favorite."

UNFULFILLING FINALE

We began Billy's final season 45-12. Rookie forward Charles Barkley was now part of the mix, and while he and Billy had their differences, he added energy and emotion to an aging cast.

But we slumped late in the year. Billy changed the lineup, starting Clint Richardson and Bobby Jones ahead of Andrew Toney and Barkley. He exploded late in a one-sided loss to Milwaukee, drop-kicking the ball into the stands. Nothing helped.

Asked by a *Boston Globe* reporter if there was a problem between the coach and players, Julius Erving said, "There's no problem that I would care to discuss." Everybody has his or her failings, Doc added. To discuss them publicly served no purpose. But then he said this: "There are some areas in which the coach is not satisfied with the team, and some areas where the team is not satisfied with the instruction. But that's something that's fairly common."

Clint Richardson told the *Philadelphia Inquirer* that if Billy were suspended in the wake of his ball-kicking episode (which he was not), "it might help [Billy] relax."

"He takes pressure, and when we lose he takes the heat," Clint said.

A reporter suggested to Billy that perhaps there was a method to his madness, that whatever abuse he was giving his team was calculated for effect.

Billy declined comment at first, then added, "We'll see."

When he looked back at that season in May 2007, he recalled that "everybody was drifting away," that the team was "splintering." So he resorted to a tactic he had often used in the past.

President Ronald Reagan, with Moses Malone looking on, is presented with a souvenir jersey during the Sixers' visit to the White House on June 8, 1983.
Philadelphia Daily News/Michael Mercanti

"My feeling was, the easiest thing to bring them together was to have them all upset with me," he said. "They'd have something in common: 'Can you believe what he's doing?'"

Whether it was because of that or not, we regained our footing in the postseason, beating Washington 3-1 in a best-of-five miniseries, then sweeping Milwaukee. But we dropped the first three games to the Celtics in the Eastern Finals. We won Game 4, then faced elimination in a familiar venue, Boston Garden.

Down by two in the closing seconds, Toney took a pass in front of our bench and did something he never did—hesitate. It was just for a split-second, as he waited to see if Billy would call a timeout. But that was all Larry Bird needed. He slapped the ball away, and time ran out—on the game, and on Billy's coaching career.

AFTERMATH

A year after retiring, Billy and theatrical producer Zev Bufman announced that they would seek to bring an NBA expansion franchise to Miami. The effort, which would include cruise line director Ted Arison and singer Julio Iglesias (among others), ultimately proved successful. The Heat began play in 1988, and Billy remained part of the organization until he was bought out six years later—save the 1987-88 season, which he spent as the lead NBA analyst for CBS.

Billy's business partners wanted him to take over as coach of the Heat in 1991, after Ron Rothstein was fired, so Cunningham did what he has always done when faced with a difficult decision: He sat down with a legal pad and listed the plusses and minuses.

And after doing so, he said, "I was still where I was in '85."

"Did I enjoy drafting players and trades and all that stuff?" he asked. "I loved it, for several years. But I had no desire to go back."

Ditto for when other teams called—as was the case, he said, until 2001. His 69.8 regular-season winning percentage is second-best of all time, just behind Phil Jackson, whose teams had won exactly 70 percent of the time through the '06-07 season.

The last two decades have seen Billy inducted into the Hall of Fame and honored as one of the 50 greatest players of all time. They have seen him celebrate the retirements of Maurice Cheeks' No. 10 and Barkley's No. 34, and mourn Wilt Chamberlain.

He now splits time between his homes in Philadelphia and Florida.

HAROLD KATZ

He traded Moses Malone. He traded Charles Barkley. He thought very seriously about trading Julius Erving—twice. He also drafted Shawn Bradley, and threatened to move the team to Camden, New Jersey. And yet Harold Katz did the one thing no owner of a major franchise has been able to do in the last quarter-century in Philadelphia—deliver a championship.

CHAPTER 22

"I don't think enough people remember that or give him credit for that," the *Daily News*' Phil Jasner said.

"His legacy should be more positive," John Nash said. "Without his desire to succeed, we might not have been able to climb that mountain."

A longtime season-ticket holder, Bryan Abrams believes Katz was "good and bad. Good in the fact that he would have done anything to win. . . . The bad thing was, he thought he was a great talent evaluator."

Don Benevento of the *Camden Courier-Post* regards Katz as "an outstanding businessman."

"People have the impression Katz was cheap; he really wasn't," Benevento said. "He was willing to invest money in the team. I just don't think he was a basketball expert. He absolutely wanted to win. He just didn't know how to go about doing it."

Katz's 15-year stewardship ended on March 19, 1996, when after considerable prodding from Pat Croce—once the Sixers' strength and conditioning coach, and soon to be the team's president—he sold the team to Comcast Corporation. It was, Katz said, "a sad day." He tried and failed to inform the staff three times, but could not; he kept breaking down. Finally, on the fourth attempt, he delivered the news.

"I was only in this business for one thing, and that was to win," he told the *New York Times*. "If I made mistakes, if I didn't do some things right, it was never done for the wrong purpose. It was done because I was too impatient to win."

The first several years of his tenure had been fine, he said. But the losing gnawed at him.

"Winning was everything to me, not making money," he said. "Pro basketball is not a regular business, and losing is not fun. I was very fortunate. I got in at the right time, and sold at the right time."

Jasner will remember Katz as always being out front, as a guy who never dodged the media.

"You didn't always agree with everything he said, but that was OK; he was the owner," Jasner said. "He always did what he thought was right, sometimes to a fault. He was always out there. He never hid."

And he always said exactly what he believed. "Harold Katz told the truth," *Delaware County Daily Times* columnist Jack McCaffery said. "If you asked Harold Katz something and he gave you an answer, that's what the truth was. . . . You could go to the bank with Harold's word. He didn't have varnish on it. There was no spin. He was the no-spin zone before there was a no-spin zone."

But Harold's straightforward approach sometimes worked to his detriment. In Nash's view, Harold was "a public-relations nightmare," who might have been regarded much differently if he had held his tongue more often.

Harold agrees that he was "too open" with reporters at times. "And as I look back," he said, "there are many things I wish I hadn't said."

He had much greater regrets than that, however. The greatest of all, he has often said, was trading Charles Barkley to Phoenix after the 1991-92 season for Jeff Hornacek, Tim Perry, and Andrew Lang.

Barkley wanted out, and tried to be as disruptive as possible throughout his final season. Still, Katz said, "I shouldn't have allowed Charles to force me to trade him. That's not me."

There was not much interest in Barkley, probably because everybody knew he had backed management into a corner.

"We made the best deal we could with Phoenix," Harold said, "but it wasn't a good deal."

The deal Katz made with Comcast was much sweeter. Having once paid $12 million for the franchise, he received ten times that.

He missed the NBA his first year out, but quickly moved on. He has since become a venture capitalist, investing in such things as weight-loss clinics, residential housing in England, and senior homes.

"I still watch the games," he said, "but have no desire to get back in."

23

Marc Iavaroni was introduced as the head coach of the Memphis Grizzlies on May 31, 2007, 24 years to the day after the Sixers secured the 1982-83 championship.

"That was a pinnacle [in 1983]," he said. "This is a base camp." Which effectively made him a Sherpa, trying to lead the Grizzlies, 22-60 in '06-07, on the long climb back to respectability.

Iavaroni saw the last of his five seasons as a Phoenix Suns assistant end with a bitter defeat to San Antonio in the Western Conference semifinals, one that was due at least in part to the fact that two Suns players, Amare Stoudemire and Boris Diaw, were suspended after leaving the bench area during an on-court altercation at the end of Game 4.

While Iavaroni had been unable to hold Stoudemire back—and he'd tried—his own fortunes had taken off long before that. Time and again he was mentioned as a candidate for head-coaching vacancies. A Portland newspaper even reported in June 2005 that he had been hired by the Blazers, which turned out to be false. Iavaroni interviewed for the position, but it went to Nate McMillan.

So Marc continued to do the same sort of dues-paying he had been doing since his playing career ended in 1991 with the last of two post-NBA seasons overseas. First he coached at the college level, then under Mike Fratello in Cleveland, then Pat Riley in Miami, and finally Mike D'Antoni in Phoenix.

D'Antoni, once a star point guard in Italy (where Iavaroni had been his teammate for a time), had installed a free-wheeling, fast-paced offense after the Suns hired him in 2003, one that clicked when Steve Nash arrived via free agency a year later. Iavaroni's role was to convince everyone that maybe they'd want to guard people once in a while. And by '06-07, they had begun to listen.

"In the past, everyone was so enamored of our offense that they kind of laughed off the need for defense," he said. "Mike D'Antoni has done a great job of understanding this is important."

Iavaroni interviewed with us in Orlando, as well as in Memphis after the Spurs eliminated the Suns. But it was the Grizzlies who made an offer.

"It happened at the right time and in the right place," he said. "I feel better about it. I got another year under my belt, another year of figuring out what I want to do as a head coach."

It wasn't quite the same as when he made the Sixers in 1982. Then *Inquirer* beat writer George Shirk told him in training camp that he had secured a spot, and Marc refused to believe it.

"In this case, it's much more believable," Iavaroni said. "I've earned it and done the right things to get to this point."

COACHES 'R' US

One week before the Grizzlies hired Iavaroni, Clemon Johnson signed on as the head man at Alaska-Fairbanks, after years of coaching high school ball in Florida, as well as in the ABA.

Two other '82-83 alums also found their way into coaching: Mitchell Anderson, who served as a pre-Iavaroni assistant in Memphis (where he worked with Lionel Hollins), after a long playing career overseas; and Earl Cureton, who worked in the ABA as a head coach and in the WNBA as an assistant.

Earl became the only player from the '82-83 club to earn a subsequent championship ring, when the injury-riddled Rockets signed him out of the CBA late in the '93-94 season.

"I felt good about it because I made a contribution [as a reserve, early in the playoffs]," Earl said. "It made me feel good that I earned my ring, that I wasn't a guy along for the ride."

Reggie Johnson coaches AAU ball outside Atlanta, where he works for an alternative school.

Franklin Edwards has kept his hands in the game, serving as a commentator on college basketball games for Fox Sports Midwest and Fox Sports Ohio.

Russ Schoene, who missed out on the championship, won three playing in Italy. "At the time," he said, "I was the winningest foreigner in the Italian League." He later settled in the state of Washington, working in construction and real estate.

THE ROAD LESS TRAVELED

Mark McNamara was on track to become an NBA assistant, too. As an advance scout and part-time big-man coach for the Toronto Raptors in 1997, it seemed only a matter of time before he assumed a full-time position.

But then the headaches and stomach problems returned, as did the feelings of general malaise. They had been part of his life since he was 15, when after being bitten by a mosquito he was afflicted with encephalitis. The symptoms had never really gone away, not even when he was playing. But there were times when they were worse than others, and this was one of those times.

His doctors were blunt. Take a year off, they said, or you're going to be dead in two months.

So he retreated to a "very woodsy" cabin in the mountains of Northern California, where he helps out the park rangers and the ski patrol. He ventures off the mountain on occasion to work as a freelance big-man coach, but he does it only when he's sure the player or players in question "want to be helped." That was true of Robert Swift, whom McNamara tutored while Swift was in high school in Bakersfield. He was chosen 12th overall in the 2004 NBA draft, by Seattle.

But generally, McNamara stays out of the mainstream. And he prefers it that way.

"I was forced to change my lifestyle," he said. "Other than the sick part, it was the best thing that ever happened to me."

"I LOVED THAT MAN"

They found Jack McMahon's body in a Chicago hotel room early on the morning of June 11, 1989. He was lying in bed, a paperback novel opened across his chest. The phone was off the hook.

The super scout died in his sleep, and in his element. Then working as the Golden State Warriors' player personnel director—a position he had assumed after leaving the Sixers when I did, in June 1986—he was in town for a predraft camp when a heart attack took him.

He left behind a wife and three children. And virtually no enemies.

"I loved that man," said John Kilbourne, the one-time strength and conditioning coach.

"When he died, I was just crushed," George Shirk said.

"I think everybody was fond of him," his widow, Kay, recalled years later. "He was a lovable guy."

She had met him when they were 16 and growing up in Brooklyn. They went to neighboring high schools and neighboring colleges, marrying in 1951, when Jack was a senior at St. John's.

A year later he began an NBA career that stretched across 37 years, and she followed him to Rochester and St. Louis, where he played, and Chicago, Cincinnati, San Diego, and Pittsburgh, where he served as a head coach. And finally, they wound up in Philadelphia, where they remained for the better part of 14 years.

She marveled at the way he immersed himself in his work, whether he was chasing Celtics star Bill Sharman around screens during his playing days or bird-dogging a prospect at some backwater college in later years.

"I don't feel like I'm working," he told her once. "I enjoy it so much that it doesn't feel like work."

After his death, she received dozens of letters from players he had coached, people he had touched.

"I don't know of anybody who was loved by everybody the way Jack McMahon was loved by everybody," Billy Cunningham said.

ECHOES

Chuck Daly, by then a highly successful coach for the Detroit Pistons, received word of Jack's death in Los Angeles, after the Pistons beat the Lakers to take a 3-0 lead in the Finals; they would complete the sweep two days later, en route to the first of two straight championships.

Immediately Chuck thought about the way Jack taught him the league back in 1977, when he was a wet-behind-the-ears assistant on Billy's first staff. He remembered driving to the Spectrum together with Jack from their homes in Cherry Hill, New Jersey. He remembered that on occasion they would raise a glass or two.

Now Chuck was two days away from a title. He wanted to feel good. But that was pretty tough to do.

MORE ECHOES

Jack was also remembered fondly when Charles Barkley was voted into the Basketball Hall of Fame in 2006. Jack saw Charles when he was a roly-poly freshman at Auburn and had liked his game immediately, calling him "a ball-handling Wes Unseld." A talent that unique could not and should not be ignored, Jack had said.

Barkley, whom we drafted fifth overall in 1984 (with a pick we had received years earlier from the Clippers in exchange for World B. Free), always appreciated that, even telling the *Philadelphia Inquirer* in the days leading up to his induction that Jack was "the first guy who gave me confidence in myself."

"[Jack] told the Sixers, 'If y'all don't draft this kid, you're going to screw up your whole future,'" Charles said.

Charles was, of course, every bit as unique as Jack thought he would be—and then some.

AN EMPTY SEAT

Further heartache awaited Kay McMahon; in 2005, her daughter Katherine died after a long battle with cancer.

She was the middle child, younger than Jack Jr., who served in the Philadelphia district attorney's office for years and is now a lawyer in private practice, and older than Brian, a computer analyst.

Jack had always doted on Katherine.

"I'm glad he didn't see her [during her illness]," Kay said, knowing how difficult it would have been for her husband to deal with his daughter's failing health.

Jack cared deeply about about everyone, which is why even now, he is still missed so much.

24

The climb was long, the stay at the summit brief. That makes it difficult to assign the 1982-83 76ers their rightful place in NBA history. They did not "'peat and 'peat and 'peat," as Moses Malone told Billy Cunningham in the champagne-soaked visitors' locker room of the Forum late on the night of May 31, 1983.

Moreover, they came along during the Magic Johnson-Larry Bird Era. Johnson's Lakers won five championships in the '80s, Bird's Celtics three. The Sixers were a blip by comparison.

There is also some debate as to whether the '82-83 Sixers were even the best team in franchise history, much less among the best in league history. The Wilt Chamberlain-led '66-67 team—a team that went 68-13 and had Billy Cunningham as its sixth man—might have been better.

But longevity, or the lack of it, is the biggest issue.

A DIFFERENCE OF OPINION

In the view of *Sports Illustrated*'s longtime NBA writer, Jack McCallum, the '82-83 club was "the best of the one-year wonders." Or, as the *Chicago Tribune*'s Sam Smith said, "as great a shooting star as any."

The *Boston Globe*'s Bob Ryan employed a different metaphor to express the same idea. Those Sixers were, he said, "like a violent tsunami that washed across the league. Moses was the man, and forced them to play with a controlled fury. For that one season the Sixers were a wonderfully meshed unit. Then the tide went back out."

Veteran coach Del Harris said, "For one year they were the best and have a place with the best."

For one year.

Sam Smith said, "They were the greatest, most overlooked team ever." But not, Smith argued, among the greatest. "When you rank a Top 10, they get bounced out because they didn't have the longevity. If they had that team together for a long period of time, it could have been a dynasty team."

Others beg to differ. Dick Weiss of the *New York Daily News* (and formerly of the *Philadelphia Daily News*) said the '82-83 Sixers were "the best team of the decade."

"It gets lost in the '80s because of the great rivalry between L.A. and Boston," he acknowledged. "Had they gone deep the next year or won, that team would be given a lot more attention."

But they did not. Still, Weiss said, "That was the last time I saw people be totally unselfish."

THE GREATEST OF ALL TIME?

Joe Axelson, for many years an executive with Kansas City and Sacramento, takes the debate one step further, arguing that the 82-83 Sixers were "the best team in the history of the NBA."

"And I have seen them all," he added. "I started out in the mid-'40s paying 50 cents to sit in the third deck of the Chicago Stadium, then the home of the world's greatest pipe organ and the loudest building ever built."

Axelson said those Sixers stand alone because of the team's guard play and free-throw shooting, as well as Moses Malone's offensive rebounding.

USA Today's David DuPree, who in 1982-83 worked for the *Washington Post*, agrees.

"People ask me about the greatest NBA team of all time," he said." I tell them I've seen some great ones, but my first choice has to be the 1983 76ers. I think of Bobby Jones' defense, Andrew Toney's laser shots, Mo Cheeks' steadiness, Dr. J's flair, and Moses Malone, the inventor of blue-collar basketball and the best ever at rebounding and scoring as a combination.

"The 76ers in '83 had no weaknesses. They had two great perimeter defenders in Bobby Jones and Mo Cheeks, which is rare. They had Doc, Toney, and Moses, who all needed the ball, but they were still a very unselfish team. It was an once-in-a-lifetime situation."

Dave Wohl, an assistant with the '82-83 Lakers, agrees the Sixers "didn't have a weakness," but stopped short of slapping a best-ever label on them. He did say they were "one of the best teams of all time," however.

McCallum noted that the '82-83 Sixers had one of everything—"the classic point guard, the classic shooting guard, a super, super center. . . . They were just a perfectly constructed team."

And they were on a mission, one that ended with what McCallum called "the ultimate verification of Julius Erving."

Even Don Nelson, who before his long coaching career played on some of the great Celtics teams of the '60s (the teams built around Bill Russell), said those Sixers "were right up there with anybody you want to talk about." He said that includes the Russell teams, the Bird teams, the great Laker squads, anybody.

"In fact, maybe they are the best ever," Nelson said. "Imagine going through the playoffs and losing only one game. Incredible."

That feat went unmatched until the 2000-01 Lakers won 15 of 16 postseason games. Their only loss? To the Allen Iverson-led Sixers in Game 1 of the Finals.

Eighteen years earlier, the Sixers did not have their expected playoff meeting with Boston. They met a Lakers team in the Finals that was crippled by injury.

Weiss said they would have won the title even if that had not been the case. "But they would have gotten a lot more credit," he said.

Hubie Brown, the Hall of Famer who coached the Knicks against the Sixers in that year's postseason and has since gone on to a successful career as an NBA television analyst, has little patience for the what-if game.

"You can do that every year, so why do it that year, to take away from that group?" he asked. "All that group could do was beat the people in front of them. Why should you emphasize missing key people? I don't get into that crap."

As Jack McCallum said, "That year they could have kept on playing until August and no one would have frickin' beat 'em."

Neil Funk would not argue the point. But as good a team as that one was, he believes he has seen better. That's because Funk, the radio play-by-play voice for the Sixers during the championship run, went on to serve in the same capacity for the Chicago Bulls. In the Windy City he described the exploits of no fewer than six title teams, the best of those the 1995-96 club, which won a record 72 games.

No team quite measures up to that one, he said. But in his career, which stretches back to the 1976-77 season, the '82-83 Sixers are "definitely in the top five, and maybe higher."

That's because of their defense, and because they were good on the road, winning 30 of 41 games. Those two things, he said, often go hand in hand.

"If you look at the great teams," he said, "they're teams that can have bad shooting nights and still win."

For that and many other reasons, George Shirk, the *Philadelphia Inquirer*'s beat writer in '82-83, said he would put those Sixers against anybody.

"Who's better?" he asked. "I remember them as the best team I ever saw."

THE MAGICAL DECADE

"The championship teams of the '80s were the greatest of all time," sportswriter George Shirk said. "They combined selflessness with physical strength and with the ability to play above the rim. And they played with a joyfulness that didn't take away from the seriousness of winning a title."

The party ended too soon for the Sixers. The decade was defined by Bird and Magic.

"Julius Erving became a backstage player to that," Shirk said. "He was lost in the shadows. He was a very Shakespearean kind of guy."

REMARKABLE CHEMISTRY

In the minds of some, the '83 team must share top billing on the franchise's marquee. Harvey Pollack, the Sixers director of statistical information and a guy who has been part of the league as long as there has been a league, said the 1966-67 Sixers—a team that had Hall of Famers in not only Wilt and Billy but Hal Greer—were the better team.

But Weiss believes the '82-83 squad had "the best chemistry of any Sixers team."

"And that includes the Wilt team," Weiss said. "I really loved the chemistry on that ('83) team. People would have regarded them even better if they hadn't lost to the Nets."

Billy Cunningham agrees that that team had "a special bond," and that it was "quite different" from the '66-67 club. But he said the two teams were similar in that both were powered by dominant big men.

He is not about to say which one he feels is better, though.

"I just feel privileged," he said, "to have been part of both of these remarkable 76ers teams."

ACKNOWLEDGMENTS

With deep appreciation, I would like to acknowledge the support and guidance of the following people who helped make this book possible.

Special thanks to Alex Martins, Bob Vander Weide, and Rich DeVos of the Orlando Magic. Thanks also to my writing partner Jim Denney for his superb contributions in shaping this manuscript.

Hats off to four dependable associates: my assistant, Latria Graham; my trusted and valuable colleague, Andrew Herdliska; my longtime adviser, Ken Hussar; and my ace typist, Fran Thomas.

Hearty thanks also go to my friends at Sports Publishing LLC. Thank you all for believing that we had something important to share and for providing the support and the forum to say it.

And finally, special thanks and appreciation go to my wife, Ruth, and to my wonderful and supportive family. They are truly the backbone of my life.

—Pat Williams

This book is the product of the memories of hundreds of people who generously shared their stories. The authors are profoundly grateful to every one of these people: Mike Abdenour, Bryan Abrams, Alvan Adams, Mark Aguirre, Danny Ainge, Toni Amendolia, Mitchell Anderson, Harvey Araton, Joe Axelson, John Bach, Greg Ballard, Gene Banks, Charles Barkley, Marlene Barnes, Dick Bavetta, Don Benevento, Kent Benson, Bill Bertka, Henry Bibby, Bernie Bickerstaff, Larry Bird, Otis Birdsong, Rolando Blackman, Fran Blinebury, Irv Block, Terry Boers, Junior Bridgeman, Hubie Brown, Larry Brown, Mike Bruton, Quinn Buckner, M.L. Carr, Bill Cartwright, Harvey Catchings, Maurice Cheeks, Mitch Chortkoff, Dr. Michael Clancy, Jerry Colangelo, Lester Conner, Michael Cooper, Dave Cowens, Joe Crawford, Ron Culp, Billy Cunningham, Earl Cureton, Chuck Daly, Adrian Dantley, Debby Davies, Brad Davis, Johnny Davis, Darryl Dawkins, Carroll Dawson, Ron Dick, Ray Didinger, Al Domenico, Eddie Doucette, Larry Drew, Mike Dunleavy, T.R. Dunn, David DuPree, Jim Durham, Mark Eaton, Franklin Edwards, Wayne Embry, Alex

English, Tom Enlund, Julius Erving, Howard Eskin, Bill Fitch, Chris Ford, Phil Ford, Jim Foster, World B. Free, Neil Funk, Dorothy Gabriel, John Gabriel, George Gervin, Matt Goukas, Mike Glenn, Mike Gminski, Jim Gray, Kevin Grevey, Darrell Griffith, Ernie Grunfeld, Bill Hanzlik, Del Harris, Randy Harvey, Elvin Hayes, Tommy Heinsohn, Mark Heisler, Don Henderson, Gerald Henderson, Rod Higgins, Sonny Hill, Stan Hochman, Lionel Hollins, Phil Hubbard, Marc Iavaroni, John Isenberg, Dan Issel, Phil Jasner, Clemon Johnson, Dennis Johnson, Eddie Johnson, Marques Johnson, Reggie Johnson, Roy Johnson, Steve Johnson, Bobby Jones, Caldwell Jones, K.C. Jones, Eddie Jordan, Harold Katz, Steve Kelley, Clark Kellogg, Greg Kelser, John Kilbourne, Albert King, Billy Knight, Bart Kofoed, Doug Krikorian, Mitch Kupchak, Bob Lanier, Fred Liedman, Alton Lister, Bill Livingston, Jere Longman, Dr. Stanley Lorber, Kevin Loughery, John Lucas, Allen Lumpkin, Jim Lynam, Bill Lyon , Jack Madden, Rick Mahorn, Moses Malone, Tim Malloy, Rollie Massimino, Cedric Maxwell, Bob McAdoo, Jack McCaffery, Jack McCallum, Jon McGlocklin, Kevin McHale, Brian McIntyre, Billy McKinney, Kay McMahon, Mark McNamara, Al Meltzer, Jeff Millman, Fred Mitchell, Steve Mix, Doug Moe, Paul Mokeski, Sidney Moncrief, Calvin Murphy, John Nash, Calvin Natt, Don Nelson, Tom Nissalke, Jake O,Donnell, Mike O,Koren, Louis Orr, Scott Ostler, Jim Paxson, Ricky Pierce, Harvey Pollack, Paul Pressey, Jason Quick, Kurt Rambis, Leo Rautins, Clint Richardson, Pat Riley, Doc Rivers, Liz Robbins, Les Robinson, Truck Robinson, Jimmy Rodgers, Tree Rollins, Lorenzo Romar, Jeff Ruland, Ed T. Rush, Bob Ryan, Gerry Ryan, Alex Sachare, Danny Schayes, Russ Schoene, Jeff Schultz, Todd Shaner, Dan Shaughnessy, Clayton Sheldon, George Shirk, Purvis Short, Gene Shue, Jerry Sichting, Jack Sikma, Paul Silas, Sam Smith, Ricky Sobers, Steve Solms, Jim Spanarkel, Rory Sparrow, Lyle Spencer, Steve Springer, Brendan Suhr, Jack Swope, Joe Tait, Laurie Telfair, Reggie Theus, Art Thiel, Isiah Thomas, David Thompson, Mychal Thompson, Rod Thorn, Andrew Toney, Kelly Tripucka, Terry Tyler, Darnell Valentine, Kiki Vandeweghe, Danny Vranes, Wally Walker, Donnie Walsh, Bill Walton, Dick Weiss, Bill Werndl, Jerry West, Mark Whicker, Lenny Wilkens, Dominique Wilkins, Bobby Wilkerson, Jamaal Wilkes, Buck Williams, Herb Williams, Bill Willoughby, Brian Winters, Dave Wohl, Mike Woodson, and Marc Zumoff.

Special thanks to *Philadelphia Daily News* sportswriter Phil Jasner, who through his relationships with both authors ensured that this project would get off the ground, then offered constant support and encouragement throughout the creative process.

Thanks to the following people for their assistance along the way: Joe Amati, John Black, George Blaha, Brian Blank, Shonn Brown, Henry Clay, Julie Fie, Karen Frascona, Brian Gleason, D.C. Headley, Bill Kline, Keith Larsen, Michael Mercanti, Stacey Mitch, Mark Perner, Lara Price, and Zelda Spoelstra.

And most of all, thanks to my wife, Barb, and son, Ryan, for their love, understanding, and inspiration.

—Gordon Jones

Pat Williams
c/o Orlando Magic
8701 Maitland Summit Boulevard
Orlando, FL 32810
Phone: (407) 916-2404
pwilliams@orlandomagic.com
Visit Pat Williams' website at:
www.PatWilliamsMotivate.com

If you would like to set up a speaking engagement for Pat Williams, please write Andrew Herdliska at the above address or call him at 407-916-2401. Requests can also be faxed to 407-916-2986 or emailed to aherdliska@orlandomagic.com.